CONNECT WITH YOUR GOD SELF

Maureen Moss

SIDNEY HOUSE PUBLISHING

Published by
SIDNEY HOUSE PUBLISHING
2305-C Ashland St. Suite 405
Ashland, OR 97520

Moss, Maureen (Maureen Cheryl)
Connect With Your God Self / by Maureen Moss
ISBN: 0-9717971-5- 3

1. Self-realization.   2. Spiritual Life.   3. Love   I. Title

Page composition/typography/cover design: Lisa Bonnice
Cover art: Debi Westbrook

Printed in USA

ALSO BY MAUREEN MOSS

BOOKS:

Commitment to Love:
Transforming Human Nature into Divine Nature

The Nature of Bliss:
Balance, Love, Integrity, Sexuality, Soul

God's Promise

Cds:

Transformation

Cosmic Wisdom

How A Powerful Woman Awakens

The Hierarchy Takes You to the Heavens

The 5 Contemplations of Bliss:
Balance, Love, Integrity, Sexuality, Soul

www.maureenmoss.com

email: maureen@maureenmoss.com

Table of Contents

Introduction 7

The Hierarchy Takes You To The Heavens................ 13

Transformation.. 37

How A Powerful Woman Awakens............................ 71

Cosmic Wisdom 95

The Five Contemplations Of Bliss 121

Introduction

L ike all of my writings, what you are about to read
was guided by Higher Realms of Consciousness,
which includes the One I refer to as God.

After being 'prompted' to put a series of five
transformational CDs out into the world, "The Hierarchy
Takes You To The Heavens," "Transformation," "How A
Powerful Woman Awakens," "Cosmic Wisdom" and The
Five Contemplations of Bliss," people world-wide asked
if I would put into writing the words to each.

The spoken words prove to be a powerful elixir for
shifting into a heightened state of consciousness. So
powerful, I was told, that people wanted to carry the
words, the prayers, and the mantras with them, as

reminders of how to connect with their God Selves, their authentic natures and Mastery of daily life.

Knowing how powerful the frequency of the spoken word is, I am also aware of the powerful frequencies of the written word and how they travel inside of us, when they are encoded in a particular way.

We are entering turbulent times and we must know how to rise above the turbulence no longer being spectators or victims. We require the tools, the prayers, the mantras, and information directly from the Hierarchy regarding the ways in which to be empowered.

Having the CDs in tandem will serve you well as companions to this book. However, having this book alone will guide you, through the written word, to rise up to meet your God Self.

I pray that you will be moved in the deepest part of your soul to re-member your true nature and—to move from the perspective of fear and doubt—to the perspective of love and courage.

In order for you to reach a higher level in your life, you are called upon to remember the importance of intention and passion, backed by *action*. Only then will you wake up to the truth of who you really are—a spiritual being, a child of God, no longer diminished by the human lies you have been told by yourself and others.

We have spent lifetime upon lifetime with very little progress of the soul. Our preoccupations have precluded our enlightenment. Most people leave the planet with such a small amount of soul growth that when they reemerge in human form they experience the same pitfalls again, only played out in a different scenario. That is not the plan this time. The plan is for you, me ... We ... to get off of the Karmic wheel and live as free beings in higher dimensions. We must use greater tools, our Higher Mind and open hearts, to free ourselves

Before you delve further into the book I'd like to offer this prayer, given to me by Spirit. There are many more throughout the book that will shift your consciousness, however let us start here. As I write these words, it is done on your behalf. Please take them deeply into your heart.

Begin by taking three deep breaths. Place your right hand over your heart while taking three slow and steady breaths in and out, in and out, in and out.

Notice yourself connecting to your heart's energy by your breath. This is the place within you where fear cannot exist. This is this place where you are guided to go when fear attempts to make its way into the temple of your being. With your breath and in your heart is where you connect to your God Self. Read the words silently first, and then lovingly speak them out loud.

"From The Light of God that I AM I call forth all of the Highest Beings of Love and Light from all levels of creation. I ask that you stand before me, as I stand before you, to claim my victory and my freedom from the illusions that have held me captive and in fear.

"I call forth protection, clarity and strength from Archangel Michael, Archangel Zadkiel and Archangel Metatron and their Legions of Light along with my I AM PRESENCE. I rise up strong and fearless this moment without interference on any level of Creation, mine or another's.

"I ask that each atom, each cell, each strand of my DNA, each bloodline that I am connected to immediately be filled with Pure White Light and peace, casting all impurities from my body, mind and spirit.

"I command that my Spirit, my heart and my mind on all levels of Creation, be illuminated and expanded to shatter all veils of illusion, Now.

"And so it is with intention set and held that I am charged by the healing ray of Love and I am lifted into the victory of my Ascension for I Am That I Am, I Am That I Am, I Am That I Am. And so be it."

Words carry power. Feel the power. Be the power. Know you carry the power of God in you. Use it over fear all of the time. Use this book and all of its distinct five parts to lift yourself into the glory of who you really are.

Come to understand where the pitfalls are, so you can walk around them or fly above them. Learn the strategies of Power, no longer held hostage by the lower mind. Re-set your mind, for you are capable. Rebirth your Consciousness, because you can. And know you are loved.

I invite you into another prayer to uplift you to your God Self. Prepare yourself as you did for the prayer above. Always prepare yourself before you call forth any prayer. Sincerely, deeply and fully use the power of the spoken word, wisely.

"From The Light of God That I Am I call forth all of my energies in outer concentration to submit immediately to the Great God Flame within my heart. I raise my perceptions and my consciousness above my mortal mind and ego to match and mirror the mind of the Great I Am that I Am. I ask that I may clearly see beyond the regions of this fear facing me and be lifted above my despair immediately.

"I Am prepared, by my word and my heart, to have God's Truth shine into my Mind transmuting every perception brought about by my human nature. By my word and my heart I acknowledge and embrace what appears to be fear and I bless it and I leave it as I move upward into the Mind of God to assess my current experience, extract its blessing, embrace its blessing and move on. And so it is, and so I let it be."

Come inside the pages of this book, listen to the CDs if you are able and prepare to glide through the times ahead.

Namaste

The Hierarchy Takes You to the Heavens

*T*his message comes directly to you from the illumined beings of Love and Light that are working diligently on our behalf to assist us in our transformation from Human Nature To Divine Nature, and so that we may arrive with grace into the fifth dimension. Please take this message deeply into your hearts, as I have mine.

Namaste, Beloveds. We honor you as Creator Gods in the midst of experiencing the Great Fallen Illusion and the return of the Light. We have both keys and meditations to offer you as you make your way toward the Heaven of your lives.

We must tell you that you are looked upon and loved dearly as some of the most respected and courageous of all of God's Creations throughout all of time. We remind you that by choice you descended to Planet Earth, the mainland of negation, to live and serve as heroes in what some may call the transition stage while others call it the ascension. The ascension stage is more accurate since you are moving upward to merge with your higher I AM Presence, your greater self. Your redemption is close at hand, though we tell you even we are ill-equipped to honor you sufficiently for what you have all agreed to.

We know the courage it took for you to descend willingly into the tides of separation, further compounded by grids of fear, force-fields of ego control and enemy patterning. We know the pain you have endured of diverted dreams and we know what each and every one of you has been subjected to by the unrelenting ego in the lower realms of consciousness.

We know the depth of love you hold for the Divine to agree to be bound for centuries by the effects of a fear-based mass consciousness and an inrush of unhappiness caused by an intensification of the outplaying of the lower human nature. Additionally you are now experiencing discomfort as your physical body undergoes the mechanics of rewiring and amplifying your unique human frequency that will enable you to hold and emit more Light and more of the of Christ Consciousness.

Yes, Beloveds, you are highly revered! You willingly stood in line waiting to descend and be covered by the veils of forgetfulness. You agreed to all of this to prove that in spite of living in reverse conditions of God Consciousness, you were capable of bringing a Planet and a species to Light and emerge triumphant with your love and your light blazing like the Great Central Sun — and with your Christ Minds in full control.

You, the chosen modern day disciples of the Holiest of Holies are coming closer each day. You are surrounded by vast Legions of Light from Universes and Omniverses beyond even your deepest rememberings. We ask that you do not stop in spite of the intensification of the mutations of your physical bodies and in spite of your minds and egos attempt to amplify their illusory validity.

It is necessary that we bring a few critical points of Light to you as you come closer to your victory and we bring you closer to the Heaven of your Life.

The first is that we have watched many of you switch your fascinations from the goings on and promises of the third dimension, to the goings on and promises of the fifth dimension. Though what is ahead for you is of great importance, the actions required for you to take NOW is of greater importance in preparing to live less encumbered in the New World.

It was spoken by the one you call Buddha that your actions are your only true belongings and that you cannot escape the consequences of your actions. Please take this to heart and into your every moment. Take it into your thoughts as well. Your thoughts prompt your actions as readily as your heart does. Every shift in consciousness comes with its own set of challenges. Don't exchange one trap for another. Stay fascinated only to the Divine Creator Gods that you are now. Nourish and sustain connection to your Divine natures only.

We also notice that the human nature is still grasping for solutions and we understand the problem. In the moment you have feet, minds and responsibilities in more than one dimension as the merging continues to take place. Many of you are confused on how to live your life in a new order outside of time with a new focus on what is truly important to your Spirit, not your personality, mind and ego.

Human negative emotions, primarily anger and despair, rise up in grasping ... whether for hope, solutions or for illumination. Cease grasping and you will cease suffering.

By now you must know that solutions come from a Source far above what the human mind can comprehend. Cease grasping. A wise soul is not thrown off balance because it cannot render solutions. A wise fifth dimensional soul of Divine Nature loves whatever is or appears to be from a state of assuredness that all is in Divine right order and *must* play itself out as this game of separation and mind and ego control comes to a close. Whatever is troubling you, let it run out of your mind untouched by another thought. Soon there will be nothing left but a quiet mind and a guided path. Rest assured.

We also ask that you stop running hither and yon for Truth. Truth seeks out every evolving being in all Universes past, present, future and simultaneous. It is the great I AM who holds the Lamp of Truth to guide you ever forward through your eternal Ascension through the infinite ages.

Beloveds, you never have to seek Truth through another, for it will always be wherever you are and in every experience you have, if you will turn a deaf ear to the mind and ego. Whatever your experience, solitary or otherwise, quiet yourself … open yourself to receptive observation, breathe and expand the Divine Spark of Light that lives within your heart and ask this simple question: "Was that the Truth that just visited me?" You will always be met with an answer and balance will be restored. This single action will take you closer to Heaven.

And now we discuss fear, the great mastermind of the human undoing. Fear—the misappropriation of thought to experience both past and present, and the ill-conceived notion of what will be. "Stop now," is the hark from the Illumined Beings of Love and Light that battle on your behalf for your illumination. We cannot continue to pierce your illusions of fear, as your full ascension depends greatly upon your personal confrontation with the lower nature of your personal fears and the expulsion of your former emotional body. This battle rests upon you.

Fear is a misapprehension of thought to experience and life and its purpose. Fear has become a ritual in the mortal mind of human, in regard to his/her future and harsh criticism of the past. Surrender it all immediately. It must cease or you will slip through the cracks between the world of illusion and the Kingdom of Heaven. Engage your Christ mind and stay only in the moments of the Now.

Beloved, cease pitting yourself against yourself. There is nothing wrong with you that a participatory shift in nature will not cure. You are stripping away your own dignity and the dignity of the great I AM which lives and breathes and has its expression of Life through you.

It is the core of your being that pleads with you to return to a complete state of love with yourself, not a partial state of war, and we will help you. Where you take notice of a conflicted nature, with compassion for the Divinity that resides within your flesh, please hasten to comfort yourself. Look beyond the conflict born of the mind and ego and race to your heart. You are in full capacity to dissolve conflict before it becomes insidious, because you have within you the genetics of the Power that gave you life. You and the great I AM are one. I AM that I AM. No separation.

Understand this in the deepest recesses of your heart. **You** are a sacred tone flowing through the Universe. **You** are a dispensation of God's Sacred Ray. **You** are the Divine Plan frequency that is manifesting its dominion on Earth, though you are being moved to Heaven. Enter the fifth dimension with grace ... we are waiting for you with deep gratitude.

Please allow us to give you prayers, contemplations and meditations to usher you closer to your personal Heaven. Use any or all of them to help you take proper action to return you to the present moment, to cease grasping for solutions, to rest rather than chase truth, to quickly switch from fear to love, to disengage fully from conflict and to be reminded of how deeply you are loved. Much of what we offer necessitates a quiet, uninterrupted space and your undivided attention

MEDITATION

Please use beautiful and relaxing music to bring yourself into a relaxed state. Record the words below in your own voice for this meditation if you do not have the CD. Your own words will make a strong impact on you and into you at a cellular level.

Take three deep and slow, cleansing breaths. Breathe in through your nose and exhale slowly through your mouth. Once again, take a full breath in through your nose, exhaling slowly through your mouth. Let your exhale be in equal proportion to your inhale, and now one more time. Breathe in through your nose and out through your mouth.

Breathe normally for a moment or two allowing your mind and body to come into calm repose.

Now take another deep breath in through the center of your heart, and breathe out through the base of your spine. Take that breath two more times. In through your heart, out through the base of your spine. Let each breath connect you to the heart of the Divine Mother Earth and your own Beloved heart. Once more breathe in through your heart, and out through the base of your spine. Connecting, connecting, connecting. Deeper into the heart of Mother Earth, deeper into your own Beloved heart.

Once again, return to your normal breath allowing your mind and your body to come into an even deeper, calm repose. You are in the present moment. Feel its joy.

Once again take a deep breath into the center of your heart and this time as you exhale see your heart opening into a beautiful golden ball of Light that expands around you and invites you to sit inside of it and just be.

Take one more deep breath through the center of your heart and as you exhale send your breath and your love upward to US, the Illumined Beings of Love and Light.

Relax into the center of your golden ball of Light and allow yourself to feel the peace, the love and the support that is being sent to you. Let yourself be filled in this present moment. Let yourself be loved in this present moment. This is your moment and it is always, always, always available to you. Fall in love with the present moment, for it is loving you, and holding you each time you hold it.

The present moment loves you and all that is contained within it loves you. It requires nothing of you, but to be fully present with it. No distractions. Notice how you feel. Just notice. Stay connected only to the noticing.

Take your right hand and gently place it over your heart. Take a breath of gratitude for the love and the power of the present moment. Let your heart love you. Let your heart keep you calm and present. That is the greater part of its role inside of your life—to keep you present.

Exhale gratitude through your entire body as you rest comfortably inside of the Divine Golden Light that connects you only to that which is important. Feel our love pouring over you and filling you. You are loved, Beloved One. You are loved.

Are you tempted to only be fascinated by the moment at hand? It is the only fascination you will ever need for in it contains everything you will ever need for any other moment to come.

Now return to normal breath and gently begin to open your eyes. Feel your body and come into the next present moment in peace. What you do with every next present moment is up to you. Choose well.

Contemplation about grasping for Truth

Let us give you a simple contemplation for ceasing the activity of grasping for Truth. Simply listen with your heart.

Truth, Beloveds, is something that the mind cannot contain. Truth can only expose itself to you when all personal concepts about yourself, of another, of experiences and circumstances have taken leave of your senses.

The mortal mind's sense of Truth has been accumulated from past experience and personal response. Truth has its own way of seeping into you through a quiet mind and an open heart. It comes only after the mind's struggling and searching for it concludes. If Truth comes into your mortal mind, it then becomes a singular perception of truth, not Universal Truth.

Witness for yourself the next time Truth comes to mind, it will constantly shift and change forms as your mind and ego adds or deletes personal story from it. If it comes through your heart it will remain constant.

Your key is a mental stillpoint. Truth comes upon you and enters once you have a final reckoning with the subversive actions of the mind and ego rendering them impotent in their capacity to enlighten you with Truth. Truth is more than the sum of their parts. And here is the key, Beloveds, to knowing when you have been visited by Truth. Your reality will immediately be stabilized and you will continue your journey to Heaven.

Contemplation for Fear

Let us speak for a moment about love and fear and then we will give you the spoken words to dissolve fear. We ask that you follow us to the tipping point where love wins you over and suffering dissolves.

In the majority of mortal belief systems most humans are convinced that something is wrong somewhere inside of them because life and all of its particulars have not turned out they way they "thought it would." As a result an underlying continuous stream of discontent, nervousness, and worry courses through most of your bloodstreams rendering you almost helpless in sustaining a loving internal environment for you to flourish and ascend by.

Fear is the fuel running most humans on your Planet Earth today and in order for your ascension to take place you must be completely drained of it and re-filled with love. No matter what you do, if you are not *being* love toward yourself and all of the Creators beings, it matters not what you do.

Fear and love operate from the exact same Force of energy. In a state of love that Force of energy works positively. In a state of fear that Force works negatively. You are the directors guiding that energetic force. You.

If you allow fear to win out it will cripple you and assure you another recycled human incarnation. If love wins, you ascend. Your entire creation will be validated as a labor of love.

Though many of you are convinced that love is beginning to replace your fears, that belief is a mental trick. Love is not a progressive state. It simply is. Either you allow love to govern you, or you allow fear to govern you. You, Beloved one, have elected one or the other, neither is hoisted upon you.

It has been written that, "Love and fear share the metal of the same coin." It does. And it is up to you to finally choose your side. We repeat, love is not a progressive state; it is a state of being proactive in every moment.

It is with deep respect to your current Earthly conditions that we remind you that you hold within you the power to extract yourself from any belief system that your mind has imprisoned you with about any experience you have ever had that in turn resulted in your inaccurate belief that something is wrong with you. There is not.

The inaccurate evidence that appears during the course of an experience to the mind and ego must be overcome by your desire to no longer have a self-centered relationship to it.

Everything is as it is unless you personally give it a particular meaning. Remember this, what is hot is hot and what is cold is cold. It just is unless you have made up your mind that hot is not hot and cold is not cold. And if you do, whatever you have decided becomes your reality.

Imagine if the ocean decided it was doomed every time it had a wave?

Now let us give you powerful words to speak directly to fear when it comes beckoning for you to participate in its games. For these words to be effective they must have your full devotion to them and your belief in them. This is not an affirmation; this is a declaration of Truth and a call for fear to be abolished in the instant of your sincere decree. Speak this as many times a day as needed, and then act in accordance each time that you do.

Use the force that directs fear and love wisely.

Become intimate with this decree.

From the Light of God that I AM I decree.

Nothing is wrong.

I no longer confuse experience as a road to despair.

Nothing is wrong.

I AM no longer burdened by my thoughts of any experience that I have.

Experiences do not require burden

They are simply an action of life that is inherent as a ceaseless imperative for me to evolve by.

Nothing is wrong.

I am grateful and fearless as I stand to meet my daily experiences.

I am grateful for knowing that they will come and go as the waves in the ocean.

I will not heroically practice to ceaselessly resist experiences that do not please me.

I will simply accept all experiences as part of something greater for Me.

There is nothing I must do but to be grateful, not fearful.

Nothing in the world external controls me, nor do I control it.

As of this day I withdraw my need to believe that something is wrong anywhere inside of me.

As of this day I release all discordant thoughts that would bind me to fear.

As of this day I demand that all shadows of my perception be diminished.

At this precise moment I declare that I no longer submit to fear.

And so it is, and so I let it be.

With fear abolished, Beloved One, we ask you to re-fill yourself with love. And we are here to assist in facilitating that loving act, as we journey closer to Heaven.

It is the ultimate and final key that will lift you far beyond your wildest imaginings and into the dimension of ascension. We remind you that all dimensions of Pure Love and Light await your arrival with great gratitude and many blessings for your persistence against seemingly insurmountable odds.

With fear gone and your love for Self restored your mental and spiritual capabilities along with a host of other glorious abilities and opportunities, will be expanded greatly.

You will find your companion, "wisdom," who has waited patiently for you.

You will experience your inherent alchemical powers. You will experience grace in all of her Glory. You will partake of Supreme Power in operation always.

Your passions will flower and find experiences with which to fulfill themselves while in body. You will find yourself experiencing more joy and more calm on a consistent basis, rest assured.

If that sounds too grand to be true, we remind you to remember that which created you—the true ONE through which all things are possible and to whom you are irrevocably interwoven. The One who is having experience *through* you is choosing to experience your GREATNESS NOW, not later as a representative of the One. And so it shall be done by your consent and devotion.

We have given you many keys to establishing proper rapport with yourselves and now we give you this meditation. It contains a pure message of Love that will lay wide the path for you to reunite with the Love that you are and to continue your journey to Heaven while in an earthly form.

MEDITATION

Please use beautiful and relaxing music to bring yourself into a relaxed state. Record your own words for this meditation if you do not have the CD. Your own words will make a strong impact on you and into you at a cellular level.

"From the Pure Light of God that I Am, I open to receive the Light of All that is. I call forth the Pure White Light of Christ and I know that I am surrounded and protected as I open myself to receive my love and the love of the One that created me."

Take a deep and steady breath in. You are about to meet the Holy One that lives inside the temple of your being. Exhale slow and steady.

Take another deep and steady breathe in. Envision Pure White Light entering you and let that Light reach and touch every corner of your being. Exhale slowly forming a circle around you with your breath.

Once again breathe in deeply, and let Pure White Light touch the very center of your heart where you and God meet and touch and create together. Breathe out and let the assuredness of your breath circle you. Breathe in once again and as you exhale, let the Light go as high, as wide and as deep as you can imagine it can.

In your mind's eye, while enfolded in your circle of pure White Light go to the center of your heart. Notice a small chamber there that contains within it a powerful spark of Light.

Amplify that Light with your breath.

That is the Light of the ONE PURE GOD that created you. That is God's outpost in you.

That Light inside of your heart is where the Source of your freedom lives. There is no other place you need ever go again to Source Truth, or to inflame yourself with Self-Love or to stabilize your connection to God's Love. Here you are safe from all interference.

Take another deep breath into your heart and connect to God. Exhale slowly, making room inside of yourself to allow nothing but the Presence of God to fill you.

Take one more deep breath in and connect deeper, deeper, deeper still until you and God are One. Exhale steadily into the circle of Light that enfolds you. You are safe.

Return your breath to a normal pace. Rest comfortably within yourself: there is a message about to be spoken to you from the Source of your Creation.

I AM here with you my child. I Am here.

I Am here because since the beginning of your Creation, I have entrusted you to be an expression of me and I would never leave you alone to fend for yourself.

I have always been with you, though often you have forgotten My presence.

Here in the center of your heart is where I rest, waiting for you.

Do you know how much I love you? Do you know? Do you know how proud of you that I Am?

Do you know that I love you even when you refuse to love yourself? You are never without love, though you may think you are.

I love you every single moment of every single day. I love you.

Do you remember that I promised that I would never leave you? Perhaps you have, but now that you are reminded in Present form you cannot ever forget. I am always here with you and for you. Always. And I will never leave.

You don't have it in you to anger me. You only have me in you, loving you. You don't have it in you to push Me away. For I Am permanent and I never leave you. You don't have it in you to betray, for so often you know not what you do, but I do and I know why … still I am not leaving you. What you do is not in you, it is simply of you. I AM in you and I am not leaving because I love you.

I Am aware of your every need, although our perceptions may differ at times; I have long known what you need to grow into the strongest expression of your glorious Self.

Do you think I do not hear your every cry, your every concern, your every call for resolution? I do and I answer, though it is often difficult for you to hear my reply since you turn often to your mind for solutions.

Do you know that each time you do, I do not judge you? I do not. I wait for you to turn in toward me so we can resolve all of your conflicts together. And did you know that even when you do not turn toward Me for answers, I work on your behalf to get the message through to you via all of my resources both internal and external?

Did you know that in my attempts through all things and beings external I am urging you to turn in to Me, inside of you so we can resolve the largest and smallest obstacles of Life with as little or no pain to you at all? For it is in your pain that I also suffer. As it is in your joy that I celebrate.

Do you know how much I love you or how thrilled I Am when you meet disappointment and turn it into your victory? It is I who celebrates you even when you forget to celebrate yourself.

Did you know that your will and my will were always intended to work together, not separately? I am not your Force. I AM your companion and Source for all of your love, and happiness, your peace and your joy — as are you and it is for that reason that I ask you to return to the Love of Yourself.

And when you do, your pain will be delivered to your compassion, your weakness will return to your endurance, your unrest will find repose and every question you have will be met with a truthful answer and you will see why you were the One that I chose amongst My many to express through.

Do you know how much I trust you?

I trust you with My very existence. And I trust that now that you know how much I love you, you will find yourself worthy of your own love and together we will rise up and gather all the Mighty parts of yourself that have been strewn hither and yon and together we will love you back into wholeness. That is your only purpose and it is my only purpose. And once your purpose is fulfilled together we will make your ascension.

Never forget how much I love you, never forget.

Transformation

*B*eginning now and through 2012, the metamorphosis that humanity has the opportunity to experience calls for exacting action, in order to orientate one's Self to the profundity and potential of what's ahead.

What you are about to receive are insights, exacting actions and attributes required for transformation from third dimensional human being to multi-dimensional human being.

While unfolding the following actions and attributes I was once again reminded that the path of the butterfly and the path of the human are similar. Both have taken on the assignment of gaining strength from the inside out in order that they may leave their restricted environments and fly free in a way that is bold and fearless.

Imagine the butterfly sequestered inside the tight confines of the cocoon.

Imagine if the butterfly thought it was merely the cocoon and stayed where it *thought* it was safe.

The butterfly would never know what was waiting for it on the other side of its apparent safety.

It would never kiss the tops of the trees, or dance on the petals of a rosebush, or light on the shoulder of the great human.

It would never know that a windy day would simply propel it forward and soon it would feel the sun on its wings and be surrounded by the magnificence that was previously unknown to it.

Imagine if the butterfly refused to break free from that which confines it. It would lose life force daily and never experience its intended life.

The human journey is similar.

Our physical bodies are much like the butterfly's cocoon and for a period of time a part of us lives inside the confines of it.

Imagine if we thought we were nothing more than what the Mortal Mind housed inside our physical bodies revealed to us?

Imagine if we decided to "play it safe" and never break-through into our Divine Natures and Multi-dimensional selves.

We would never know what Jesus meant when he proclaimed "these things and more shall you do!"

We would never have the courage to reach for the stars, and cavort with the angels and an array of beautiful Beings of Light that are often out of our physical sight.

We would never realize that fear is just a state to pass through, not a ball and chain. We would never dance gracefully with The Great Mystery.

We would render ourselves incapable of passing through states of consciousness that leads us to our greatness.

We would always settle for less.

Imagine if the human being refused to break free from that which confines it. The human being would lose life force daily and never experience its intended life.

The butterfly instinctively knows what's necessary for transformation. Now the human is being reminded.

Your transformation is the greatest blessing you could ever imagine.

It is indeed an unprecedented time in human evolution as we do what no other collective human species has done before. We are transforming our Human Natures into our Divine Natures without ever leaving our bodies. We are transforming our human mortal consciousness that is riddled with false perceptions about life and transforming it back into God Consciousness where the essence of our being longs to return. And, if that's not enough, by our dedicated actions, we are creating a New World sustained by Love, something that no other human species has done before.

We are being looked upon by the Highest Beings of Light as heroes in a transition stage.

I would like to remind you of something you may have forgotten.

Long before you arrived in your current human form you were determined to BE a Force of Love. You agreed to have an explosion of God Consciousness at the Divine right moment in time allowing you to become a vehicle for the force of evolution. Now it is time for your original intention to become self-evident.

Each one of you holds the capacity to be Powerful Earth Transformers and Divine Nature Sustainers. Though the task has not yet been fully accomplished you have been created to succeed, and you will as long as you allow yourself to fearlessly walk the line between the known and the unknown and embrace and utilize the insights, exacting actions and attributes to follow, if they resonate with your heart and soul now.

It is of no value for you to wait for something outside of yourselves to change and make you appear to be safe before you begin to live up to your potentials and task at hand. Doing so will only continue to stir the pot of the ever bubbling Mortal Mind in its quest to keep you from your Great Potential. That is also an action born of the lowest of human consciousness.

It is your birthright, and right timing to experience your Great Potential and the unlimited possibilities that your particular life affords you.

Throughout your transformation the Highest Most Noble Beings of Light will stand by your side to offer support, certain direct interventions, guidance, and illumination. They remind us at the same time that *we* are the agents of change, not them. (Many of these beings you will find in *Commitment to Love: Transforming Human Nature into Divine Nature.*)

It was always understood that the time would come in your current lifetime when the consciousness of the human Mortal mind and heart would be inferior to the evolution of your souls. That time is at hand.

You are in the last years of a grand cycle of human experience. This last cycle requires a grand quickening in your soul's evolution.

In order for this quickening to take place both your Mortal Mind and your human heart must go through a transformative process to accommodate your true and authentic natures while in human form.

Presently most of humanity lives their lives to merely surmount challenges largely created by the Mortal mind and the human nature. This manner of living has compromised the well being of your physical and emotional bodies, greatly taxed your Spirits and separated you from your true Divine Natures that affords you many luxuries.

You have stayed inside the cocoon of your lower human natures for a dangerously long period of time and a push from your Higher Self is forcing you out of it. It is time for you to have a true relationship to Life. It is time for you to fly.

Your transformation and reconfiguration has begun. Many of you are being confronted with unfamiliar energies causing physical and emotional upheaval. You have nothing to fear. Know that all of your bodies are acclimating to a more expanded version of who you are, so be patient.

Most of you have been out of touch with this "expanded frequency field" for a long period of time. Though many of you may feel this reconfiguration is catching you off guard, so to speak, know that it is your guarding of the old ways and means of a lower human nature and a demanding and ceaselessly grasping Mortal mind that is causing you the most discomfort. Let them go. They're old. They're toxic. They're based in fear and damaging to who you really are. Bless the old and let it go.

A way is being made for you to experience your multi-dimensional Selves with Divine Heart and Mind intact. A way is being made to end the life of your current circumstances and take you to higher ground where clarity, not confusion, love, not fear, and joy not pain abounds.

Those of Higher realms of consciousness are taking care of all things technical and electrical. They are busy re-wiring, firing, expanding and reconnecting heart chakras, global brain coding and strands of DNA along with many other energetic reconfigurations necessary for a human being to jump two dimensions in one lifetime and experience multi-dimensionality.

Your job is to purposefully open your heart at all times and open your mind. Drain out all toxic thoughts and consciously keep them out. Cultivate tranquility. Make friends with neutrality not reaction, become intimate with spiritual integrity and discernment, and create the conditions where the desires of your heart can become the reality of your being. That is key and bears repeating. **Create the conditions where the desires of your heart *can* become the reality of your being.** You will be supported at every turn.

That is the Law and The Promise of Creator Source.

Bend when you must. Pull when you must. Both are an offering. When you bend, be at peace, when you pull, do so gently.

Those in the higher realms can only be successful on their end as a result of you doing your part here and now. Everything above and below will help you significantly if you take them to heart and into action.

As human beings your complexity is far greater than you know, as is your power and your capabilities. Seek not to understand your complexities. Seek only to test all of your capabilities. That is another key to your success in your phenomenal transformational mission.

By now it is no secret that your transformation from one state of being to another demands everything from you, and then a little bit more. All of your bodies, mental, emotional, physical and spiritual are affected by your transformation. It is your job to balance and stabilize them daily through the practice of self-compassion.

The Attribute of Compassion

Compassion is an attribute of Divine consciousness. Being self-compassionate allows you to make a quantum leap in the evolution of consciousness.

Self-Compassion asks that you embrace and celebrate your capabilities and strengths, seeking the forgiveness of yourself for your life actions that you would like to avoid.

As you extend forgiveness, tenderness, warmth, and sensitivity *toward* yourself, you will find many beliefs and judgments that have kept your consciousness low, departing. Shame, guilt, and despair will literally pour out of your body, leaving room for more Light and Love to expand within you and shatter the cocoon of lower human consciousness.

Each time you choose to be compassionate with yourself, you have chosen to be more balanced, more stabilized, more of God. Each time you do not, you express yourself as a mere fraction of who you are. All of your bodies suffer greatly, taking you away from your transformation, not toward it.

You have been given many powerful allies in your lifetime to help you achieve your full Majesty or transformation. Here are two: They are experience and choice.

Experience will never work against you, unless you allow your mind and ego to interpret them. Your choices hold great power to usher you forward or to set you back. Take neither of them lightly.

Here are some further insights to quicken your transformation.

The *manner* in which you love yourselves and each other is of vital importance and is recorded daily in your cellular structure. One day that you deprive yourself of your own love will cause you a setback and a weakening in all of your bodies.

One day that you strip yourself or another of dignity will cause you a setback and a weakening in all of your bodies.

Each time you judge yourself you cause yourself a setback and a weakening in all of your bodies.

Each time you race to your Mortal mind for an answer to satisfy your ego during *any* experience you cause yourself a setback in all of your bodies and a weakening in your Spirit.

Only your pure heart and Divine Mind has the authority and ability to give you appropriate perspective about any experience leading to your transformational ascension. Here is a key: if you cannot find the blessing in your experience, any experience, your Mortal Mind and ego has interpreted it. You are being asked to bend your ear toward your heart and Divine Mind. Place your faith only in your heart and Divine Mind.

Developing faith in both will strengthen you irrevocably. Faith is another Divine Attribute.

As you journey through your transition, seed yourself with faith daily, regardless of all circumstances.

Faith is the mightiest tool ever given to humankind for transformation and for turning dreams into realities.

Faith is a belief in what can't be seen; it is knowing that the unseen exists, and acting in accordance with that knowledge.

Faith led Moses to the Promised Land, Columbus to the West Indies, and Galileo to look to the stars. Faith led to the creation of electricity; it made possible mortal man's ability to travel to the moon and walk on it. Faith is so powerful that it literally creates realities and states of minds.

When you are vigilant against the negativity and destructive power of the ego, and you hold faith in its place, you can transcend into a consciousness previously unknown. Most have believed that all things are possible through God. Soon you will discover that all things are possible through *you*, if you have the faith that this is so.

It is important to understand that Faith has two sides—negative and positive. Both are equally powerful and both are creative forces.

Partially responsible for humanity's lower consciousness has been an accumulation of negative faith, based on false beliefs arising from personal fear, or the internalization of others' negative perspectives.

False beliefs give as much life to what is believed as positive faith. Negative faith (fear) creates delusion, seeming inability, stagnation, and despair. Negative faith waits for the worst to happen.

Positive faith (deep trust) is right use of energy. It allows you to transcend the illusion of what appears to be and to appropriate a different reality, leaving time out of the mix. Positive faith is *born* from right identity and connecting to the Light of God within you, allowing a positive impression to be made in Universal consciousness. That impression allows for all possibilities to be made manifest in form. Do not confuse positive faith with delusion. Delusion is a false conviction held in spite of the invalidating facts.

There is a fine line, but a big difference.

Positive faith allows you to reach your highest expectations, if you joyfully do your part without restriction and then wait for all that is necessary to come together in Divine right time, not mortal time. As you become more aware of the fact that you *are* God made manifest in form, and stay true to the course of your evolution, then you will know that nothing born of right intention is a limitation to you.

As a human being, you have been allowed to experience freely whatever you put your faith into, positive or negative. One keeps you focused on possibilities presented to you from the mind, which automatically limits limitless potential. The other connects you to your God Consciousness, establishing a connection to all potential outcomes, those of which the human mind is incapable of perceiving.

If you are to assume your transformative Divine natures, you will be required to have faith, and you will be tested, so be aware.

There is no other way to prove to yourself that what seems far-fetched to the human mind is of no issue to the Divine mind. If you feel that you are being guided to do something out of your comfort zone, or to think outside of your human box, know that you are being asked to make a leap of faith toward something greater for yourself.

If you choose to make that leap, you will have devotional support from the unseen realm to ensure that you make it successfully to the other side. Only the human mind and ego sets you up to fail. The Divine Mind of God that asks you to step to the edge of the cliff of your comfort zone sets you up to succeed.

Faith is the foundation on which you carry the Love and the Light that you are. Faith is a matter of great importance in your transformation. Negative faith will be of no value in your transition.

Undoubtedly by now, you sense that you are more valuable than you may ever have believed. Each of your lives has a specific purpose that can only be realized through a higher state consciousness.

Have faith and be prepared.

The following two decrees will help you strengthen your foundation of faith, and connect you strongly to the Heart of God, but only if you believe and feel what you speak.

The Decree of Faith

I no longer confuse what I seem to be with who I really Am.
Knowing who I Am, I still my mind, greet my courage, and
seed myself with faith.

Transformation

Here in my solitude, I Am not burdened by thoughts of the past.

I have no fear of the future.

Divorced from past and future, I have faith that Life in all of its infinite wisdom will take care of me.

Holding positive faith, I know all situations will be resolved in Divine right order without my control.

The Consciousness that brought my Spirit here is the Consciousness that will guide me safely through my life the instant I allow it to.

My path is illuminated by Divine Light as I take each step toward my Divine nature.

Every question I have is met with an answer when I still my mind to listen.

I have faith in the power of the Love that I Am and my way is made clear.

I take each step forward with faith and love.

This moment I bind myself to positive faith and allow the power of good to surge around and through me.

I Charge myself with radiant I Am Light and embrace all power given to me from above me and within me.

My faith and courage dispel the limits and inhibitions of my past, and I intend to live each day from this moment on in faith, elevating my consciousness and being lifted into the future of myself.

I Am indeed blessed . . . and so it is.

Follow the Decree of Faith with the following Light Decree

From the Light of God that I Am, I decree the Light and I Are One.

This moment, I flood myself with Light, casting out doubts and fears as I touch every corner of my being with Light.

I honor the Light of God within.

I honor the Light of God above.

It is all One, connecting at different points, and I Am one with it everywhere.

I will not let anything come between Us.

I will stay connected to Light and Love, always.

I will no longer deny my Oneness with all of Creation.

I Am ending all bonds of darkness and separation from eternal Light and Love now — for all time.

I Am Light-filled — all weights are gone.

I Am surrounded above and below with Pure Light and Pure Love.

I Charge and I Charge and I Charge myself with radiant I Am Light.

I feel the flow of Light that now makes all things right.

All that is meant to be mine by Divine Right has Light cast
*   upon it.*
It is released to me in Divine right order, unhindered, under
*   Grace in a magical way.*
I Am Love, Light, Power, and Divine Wisdom.
And so it is, and so I let it be.

Speaking both the Decree of Faith and The Light Decree daily as an exacting action are only as good as the power behind them. The power comes when you connect to their meaning in a heartfelt manner, believe in what you are saying and doing, and commit to following through on the stated intention. I Will, I Am, and I Charge are strong words that deserve a deeper understanding.

I Will

"I Will" is a proclamation of a Godly commitment that sets up a sacred contract with whomever you have proclaimed it to. On an unconscious level many proclaim "I will" to give themselves room *not* to commit. Here's why.

The words *I will* give the speaker the *feeling* that they have already delivered what they have pledged with those words. This false sense of accomplishment brings about false gratification. Eventually, all things come into view for all to see. When what was promised by I will does not appear, discontent and disappointment set in.

If you do not follow through on your I will contract, a quiet rumble of "I'm not good enough" gains energy and spreads within you, often on an unconscious level. This darkening energy dims Light, which is wisdom and truth, amplifying lower consciousness.

To move to a higher consciousness and experience your Divine nature, it would be wise to consider the words *I will* as a sacred vow or say nothing at all. Trust cannot exist when you break promises to yourself or another. If you decree empty words, you connect to nothing.

I Am

The words "I Am" work within the planes of your inner kingdom; they establish a connection between you and Creation in the center of your heart.

I Am means that Divine Intelligence and Divine Love have merged with you personally. They are words to remind you that there is no separation. When you speak the words *I Am*, you are giving voice to your Divine Self and interlacing with the energy of God within.

I Am are words born of the highest Sacred Energy declaring something to be so. They are evocative words created to elevate the human spirit into Divine Spirit. In Truth there is no separation. I Am that I Am, translated means I Am God, I Am. The words carry a frequency that reaches into many realms of higher consciousness, and they are a summons for the laws of alchemy (the All-Chemistry of God) to manifest.

I Charge

The words "I Charge" activate your entire field of energy. Negative thoughts, fears, and everyday circumstances deplete that field. Not unlike electrical gadgets and automobiles, whose batteries are drained by usage, your energy is drained as you move through daily life.

Just as you recharge batteries, it is imperative that you recharge yourself. Getting a good night's sleep or taking a vacation is an act of human nature and, though useful, is no longer enough to charge up your Divine nature high enough to transform. To take care of yourself please stay fully and consciously charged with Light energy.

As you proclaim, believe and feel the words "I Charge myself with radiant I Am Light," you are invoking a dynamic surge of energy that sends your body, mind, and spirit a message: *The Light is on in my temple.*

Say these words over and over again. "I charge and I charge and I charge myself with radiant I Am Light. I feel the flow of Light that now makes all things right." Raise your arms to the Great Sky when you say them. Feel the energy you call forth into your body. It is magical and instantly transformative.

Take your time ingesting this information. Repeat the decrees daily. These exacting actions and insights are an extremely important part of this plan of transformation. There are many layers of human nature that must be penetrated, requiring your patience.

Here is another insight to consider. Many humans seek their awakening through machines and energetic or verbal promptings given by another that promise to clear your path to your awakened state.

Gratefully, there are many wise and technologically advanced brothers and sisters on and off of the Earth dedicated to assisting you in balancing and opening your frequency fields, your meridians, your chakra system and more. Many are capable of helping you gain higher perspectives to emotional issues. There is, however, no machine or another human being on this Planet that is capable of rendering you awakened or transformed. It is only by *your* vigilant, personal actions that you will be able to transfer into the Heaven of your Life.

Test your capabilities. There is great joy in discovering what you are truly capable of.

Here are further insights regarding love and fear to help you transform from one to the other.

Fear and love operate from the exact same Force of energy. In a state of love that Force of energy works positively and you will *see it* reflected in your life. In a state of fear that Force works negatively and you will also *see and experience that* reflected in your life. You are the directors guiding that energetic force that engages love or engages fear, *nothing* random in the Universe has that power any longer.

Use your alchemical powers to steer that energy in the direction that you wish it to go in. You are fully capable of steering energy. You have full authority to steer that energy. Test your capabilities. See how far you can stretch and reach and accomplish beyond your former belief systems.

Test your love and flow your love purposefully. Be love everywhere, in every moment, with yourself, with every person, with every aspect of Creation and with every experience you have.

You are the wayshowers of the alchemical power of Love.
Always remember The Love that you are is alchemy and when expressed, changes everything in its midst, everything. Love is the only power that exists that is not an illusion. It is the only power that can evoke permanent change.

The Love that *you are* means that you have the power to immediately rise above all personal despair and ascend beyond the limited belief system of the mortal mind. It means that you have the power to change all circumstances shadowed by darkness into pure Light.

You were created having the ability to rise above mortal understanding and tap into the wisdom and truth of God and use it in *all* circumstances to transform your life.

The Love that you are means that you carry within you peace that surpasses all mental understanding.

1. Being Love means that you have great worth. You are valued and valid as God in human form by all who see you through Divine eyes. You never have to seek worthiness through another.

2. Being Love means that you are a part of the Highest Intelligence in the Universe. It means there is nothing more you have to strive for, since there is nothing greater to be.

3. Being the Love that you are in human form at this particular time in Earth's history means that before you arrived on planet Earth you committed to changing natures when necessary. You agreed to refine and purify your emotions, resurrect your true identity, and live masterfully while still in form.

4. Being Love means that you not only hold the solution to human perils, but also the means for human joy.

5. Being Love means that you are responsible for gathering all of the parts of your fractured Self, the

parts you have abandoned or become ashamed of, and carry them tenderly to the altar of your heart for repair.

Those are but some of the blessings of knowing that you are Love, and the power that that knowledge carries. Knowing is the beginning of being.

Take action and transform the Love that you are into a mansion filled with Light—the dwelling place of God within you. Give yourself the dignity of your own love before you go seeking it from someone else. It will transform you. When you believe in yourself and love yourself, no one else has to love you. They will just want to.

As your transformational journey continues you will no doubt find yourself drawing new relationships into your life, as does the butterfly when it leaves the cocoon once and for all.

Notice that with your transformative Divine Nature and Divine Consciousness intact you will only have the desire to engage in relationships that propel you forward, nurture your soul and give you a place to amplify the God in form that you are. You will no longer choose to set up or engage in any relationships that cause you a setback. You have worked far too hard to get this far. Do not allow your Mortal mind and ego to set up any circumstances that betray you and pain you. Let your Heart and Soul lead the way, always.

Learn to interpret the language of your Soul. Unlike the Mortal Mind it speaks from an unlimited Source of Potential in a subtle, not raucous manner. It is not insistent. It is subtle in its approach.

For you to interpret the soul, you would be wise to interpret it differently than you do the Mortal Mind. Do so watchfully, quietly, with inner eyes and without a rush to judgment. Your soul will never lead you on a joyless quest.

You may notice that it will summon an unfamiliar longing in you. The longing is for peace and harmony, transparency, mutual collaboration and trust.

Your soul will request that you employ every aspect of the deepest meaning of faith, courage and surrender so you will enjoy the relationships you perhaps have dreamt of, but it remains a dream. If you listen to your soul when it comes to all relationships that you have in life you will have the opportunity to live your dreams ...

awakened. Here are several qualities of a soulful relationship.

The first is Self-Awareness.

Without truly knowing yourself apart from the ego and personality's' interpretations of who you are, you can never become vividly conscious, and call forth and engage in a soulful relationship of any kind. Remember who you are is God in form, Love in form. Let no other interpretation enter your mind.

In order to represent yourself fully to another and to interact consciously, authentically, impeccably, and comfortably in relationship with another you must be completely honest and stunningly clear about who you are and where your commitment to love and spiritual intimacy really is. Self-awareness allows you to show your unvarnished self in all of relationship's transactions, comfortably.

Next is honesty.

In a soulful relationship, the commitment to being honest is of paramount importance. If honesty does not exist or ceases to exist there will always be a crack in the heart of that relationship. We have a spiritual responsibility to telling the truth **with compassion and sensitivity**. Wherever truth is not spoken someone is being stripped of their dignity, and another precious light has been dimmed on this Planet.

Honesty, in part, is lovingly telling the truth of what you're afraid of, or what's important to you or how you feel about something spoken or implied. That level of honesty will create a bond of intimacy and depth if you have chosen your relationship at soul level.

Honesty in all relationships is the glue that holds it together or ends it. Based on past experience many people feel that honesty is too big of an emotional risk. Remember you are operating from a fearless transformed state now.

Honesty is THE catalyst for intimacy and growth. If you are being heartfully, compassionately, soulfully honest with someone and that someone turns it against you, then know this … you have been spared.

The third aspect of a soulful relationship is Vitality.
Vitality is energy. It's a barometer of your life force. It's life's juice and vigor and passion that wakes up your cells and your souls. Vitality or lack thereof is very telling about another, so pay close attention.

It's vitality that makes all things possible and opens the mind and heart to growth, and renewal and change in life and relationship.

The opposite of vitality is lethargy. All relationships that you engage in that makes it soul-worthy need to be vital, giving both involved a sense of vividness, and openness and potential. It gives each the awareness that something so good is happening here in spite of any obstacles that may be crossing your path. Without vitality in a relationship, there is no power in the journey.

Empathy is the fourth aspect of a soulful relationship.
Empathy is connecting and embracing another's hardship as your own, without being pulled down by it. We express empathy remembering at soul level there is no separation between us and our Beloveds.

Empathy does not make you responsible for another's hardship. It's not meant to create a codependency. It allows you to witness tenderly and consciously another's pain without judgment. Empathy is a quality of a soulful relationship that is elegant and refined in its nature.

It's the wellspring of compassion that arises from the level of your own soul and unites you on a deeply spiritual level. Empathy asks this question: what can I do to love you in and through this situation?

If it asks too much of your Spirit, then you have a choice to make on behalf of transformed self.

The next is Forgiveness.

In a soulful relationship forgiveness is the giving of grace and understanding to another that has consciously or unconsciously hurt us. This is often a tall order but it's imperative in our own **soul's** growth and transformation as the personality and ego departs from center stage. We have to remember that we have all hurt one another numerous times in our lives. It's part of the unconscious human experience.

In relationship we have the beautiful opportunity to measure our hearts not by our anger, or for our own well-being, but by our commitment to **offer** a second chance which in turn will allow us to be **given** a second chance. It is another aspect of our God-like natures to rise above our emotional reactions to another's behavior and respond with love, giving **them** the opportunity to expand by our love.

Forgiveness does not mean you live without boundaries, or self-respect. It means you are willing to give someone the opportunity to rise up beyond their own fears and unconscious behaviors, or not. If the same unconscious act is perpetrated once again it is your decision to know when to draw the line in the sand.

All of your soulful relationships deserve the best possible chances to succeed. When we forgive, truly forgive another, you add a thread of Light to the fabric of this Universe leading to its transformation

And finally, Gratitude.

Gratitude for our relationships is gratitude for the unfolding of the creation of the human potential. Every relationship you have is a blessing, a miracle, a gift, a teaching, if you will only stop and see them that way.

The soul is always in gratitude for the relationship at hand. It is only the personality and ego that keeps tabs and worries that the scales aren't balanced. It searches for the problems in the relationship and stops the flow of the sacredness of relationships.

Relationships teach you how to fall and get up. They teach you how to be generous with your hearts. Relationships are God's way of helping you become more of who we are and that is worth gratitude at the deepest level.

Once you become your transformed Divine Self stabilized, you are going to receive an assignment from the Universe. It is going to come right to you, and it is going to test your faith. The assignment will be a plan of action that will lead you right into what you came to planet Earth to *do* in fulfilling your mission in Life. Remember, it won't define you, for you have been defined. It will fulfill you, to be sure.

Everything you have done up to this point in your life will have prepared you for your Divine assignment. What it will be may surprise many of you, because your mind and ego will tell you that you can't do it. Please don't turn away from Divine guidance. Turn away from Mortal mind and ego as they will still attempt to insinuate themselves into your life.

Not only can you do it, you *will* do it in a transformed and Divine form! Everything you have done in your life thus far will be linked in some way to your ultimate assignment. You will look in awe at the Divine workings of your life, even those before you transformed.

Your assignment won't be given to you in full form at the beginning. It will be given in a way that is manageable for you, though you will be stretched a bit at first. You must trust what shows up, as odd as it may seem to your mind, and pursue it faithfully. In the end, it will make perfect sense, and you will be elated. It's a gift from God, I promise you that.

Enjoy Your Transformation. It's worth every step you take.

How a Powerful Woman Awakens

*O*nce upon a time, a Beloved feminine essence, you, were born into a world of infinite possibilities. Inside of you the seeds of your magnificence, your powerful magnificence, were planted.

Before you left for your Earthly sojourn God asked you to remember that the seeds of your powerful magnificence were your responsibility to harvest during your earthly lifetime *by your own love*. It was long ago ordained that the return of the shining Feminine Goddess, with all of her magnificent possibilities for herself and the world would rise up in your third millennium on Planet Earth.

With promise intact you journeyed to Earth and the veils of forgetfulness covered you as you slept. The veils have been lifted, woman, and now you are free to awaken, fully. You are free to love and be loved once you inflame your powerful self and refuse to betray yourself ever again. You are being given all of the Omniversal support from The Divine Mother aspect of God's Highest Light to love yourself fiercely, softly, and honorably, but take note—you must protect yourself from your own mind in order to awaken

As the New World pronounces itself to humanity led by The Divine Feminine, it introduces a powerful new role for the emerging powerful woman. She is clear, she is relaxed with herself, she has boldness and softness, she settles for nothing and knows that nothing is out of her reach. She keeps herself on track by her connection to her heart and the heart of The Mother/Father God that lives inside of her, she prays and meditates, she dismantles her internal Department of Defense and refuses to let the world external seduce her.

Your full power has been summoned, Beloved. There is a request by the great I AM that I Am to wake up and activate your full Divine powerful feminine potential NOW.

You can no longer invalidate the powerful woman that you are. For if you did, you would be misleading yourself and denying your true heritage. You can no longer be tyrannized nor tormented by a mind and ego that uses tricks to keep you bound to the illusion of inadequacies, unless you decide differently.

Woman, the time is upon you to reclaim your powerful magnificence, and rise up and restore yourself. Be unafraid to reveal who you really are. As a magnificent force of LIGHT your purest Self is needed in a world shadowed with illusion.

No longer a slave girl fastened to your past or your future, you are being summoned by the Holiest of Holies to climb atop the "story of your life" and take your rightful place as a powerful woman. You are the ONE you have been craving all of your life. You are the most important relationship you will ever have.

It has never been taken lightly that earth life has taxed your spirit, prompted Divine Power to leak through the pores of your skin and asked much of your heart, but take heart powerful woman, it has not robbed you of the gifts of persistence, determination and courage. Each is omnipotent. Nor has the fire of the Divine Mother God been extinguished within you. Though it may have been dimmed while in the throes of experience, you, powerful woman, are the keeper of the omnipotent flame.

Rise UP, powerful woman! Rise UP and stretch to meet your Self and you will be received with ecstatic applause.

How, you may ask, do I reach and release my powerful Self with wounds still oozing, and psyche still bleeding? How do I forsake my past, nourish my tired body and silence my mind that often berates me and tears at my essence?

You must know this, powerful woman. As the veils of illusion are lifted by your actions you will come to know that your weakened "sense of self" has been an illusion created by all false beliefs held in regard to the mental perceptions of the experiences of your life.

First, powerful woman, you make the choice to reclaim yourself. Choice is your ally and constant companion. Use it well. Treat it in a holy way. Every moment of your existence is a choice. You are but a choice away from living your life the way you and the Highest God intended it to be lived. It is up to you, blessed one, powerful one, to make the choice to turn yourself in the direction that is noble—toward your heart, away from your mind, toward your power, not your weakness, toward your now, not your next.

It is your mandate to Divine responsibility to no longer make choices in a cavalier manner regardless of the oftentimes seductive nature of poor choice. It is up to you to understand the magnitude of every single choice you make.

Though you may proclaim that you are torn between this choice or that choice, for undoubtedly many parts of yourself speak to you at the same time, know this … there is only one of you listening.

When it comes to choice, it is up to you to discern the difference between the contradictory impulses of your mind and ego and defer to your heart and soul. It is not required that you go to war with your mind or ego, simply that you disengage from their hypnotic proddings.

Your first clear choice to do so will lead you to the second way to awaken to your power.

It is for you, powerful woman, to begin to listen and interpret the language of your heart and soul, so you are shielded from trickery. It is also an imperative that you understand that the heart and soul rarely request something easy for your mind and ego to embrace.

Your mind and ego speak to you literally ... giving you rationale, reasons, pros and cons for anything and everything. Let us tell you an ill-kept secret ... the mind and ego never has a true-life experience for they already believe they know everything about any experience it has. They do not and cannot.

Neither was created to interpret nor impress upon you anything about experience. Experience is a way for you, for all of humanity, to dance with LIFE in all of its myriad forms and it is a catalyst to evolve past the ego that takes every experience as a narcissistic opportunity to create separation.

Your mind uses experience as a means to haunt you—much like a predatory ghost. Your heart uses experience to carry you to your compassionate, wise powerful self that lies in your great potential. Your heart takes what may appear to be an adverse experience to prepare you for your greatness. Your heart uses experience as a lamp unto yourself. Be unafraid to turn that lamp on.

The job of the mind and ego, in relationship to experience, is to confuse and separate you. They have only the illusion of respect for you as they band together to deplete your power with their constant stream of justifications, defenses, opinions and interferences. They use your experiences to scatter you in directions that would appear to make it impossible for you to gain clarity.

They will not allow you the rite of passage to glean the wisdom of your heart. Pay attention and you will notice this.

A powerful woman always seeks the harbor of her heart in and through each experience because she knows she will find clarity, unified peace and comfort as a result.

Learning the communication skills of the heart and soul differ greatly than those of the mind and ego. It will not take you long, powerful woman, to learn to discern the difference and serve only one unified, loving Master.

The mind and ego are insistent and raucous in their approach. The heart and soul speak subtly and abandon typical human clarity which is why, powerful woman, you must listen closely with a Divine ear, not a human one. When the heart and soul communicate to you, you will note it preserves mystery. Mystery is a sacred homestead for you, not a monster under your bed.

A life lived gracefully while in mystery is life expanded, and opened to its fullest potential. It allows the grace and majesty of the Great Mother/Father God to enter and expand inside of you with a myriad of possibilities. The goals of your heart and soul are your liberation. They offer you power and they offer you an opportunity to hone your skills in faith.

A powerful woman rests in the mystery of faith. She is at peace. She leaks no power. A woman without faith is merely a weakened slave girl, held hostage by the mind and ego. You will recognize her as she paces hither and yon for peace, always ruminating for solutions and resting every once in awhile from sheer exhaustion.

Faith is the third part of your awakening, Beloved. Faith prepares the path for your awakened Spirit to travel on.

But how do you discern the difference between *believing* you have faith and *having* faith?

You know when you need not ask the opinion of another. Faith is trust. It is not hope. It is a knowing, a deep knowing that lies in the loins of a powerful woman unmoved by the taunting of a neurotic mind and ego. Hope is not an attribute of a powerful woman for it holds a dim light that flickers on and off. On and off.

To have hope in the message of the heart and soul is no more than a querulous wish for something good to happen. Hope carries itself hunched over in a weak attempt to better your life. Cease cherishing hope and jump into the sincere space of faith. That leap will carry you past settling for mediocrity.

Faith does not live in your head. It lives in your heart and is brought to life by the gentle guidance of your soul. It is your responsibility to take whatever actions are required to give it a safe harbor to be nurtured far, far away from intrusive thoughts, or the thoughts or opinions of another.

Take a vow, powerful woman; take it one hundred times a day or a thousand times a day that you will not allow your safe harbor to be taken over by a faithless thought. Claim that harbor as a safe-haven, a refuge where only faith can enter. And stand guard, powerful woman, at the harbor of your Self to insure that no malcontents, no stray or abusive thoughts, no imposters of mind or ego can find their way in. You, powerful woman, are the keeper of the harbor. Make that a mission and you will find your power. That is another vital key.

A powerful woman has no need to understand exactly how circumstances will work themselves out. Simply feel its insistence press upon your heart that it will, and allow yourself to be patient and at peace with that.

The next stage of your awakening comes about as a result of patience. At times patience will appear demanding, for indeed it is a mighty attribute of a powerful woman. Patience requires stability. Here is another key, powerful woman. It is your quality of thought toward any and all experiences that determines stability. Breathe that in for a moment, for it is no small task. It is your quality of thought toward any and all experiences that determines your stability.

Patience asks that you stay united only with the moment at hand and if you do you will be taken to the other side of the moment unscathed. Take this to heart: You, blessed one, have already been designed to succeed, so be patient.

The sign of an impatient woman is one who is reactive to both external and internal changes, causing instability and internal frenzy resulting and lessening herself to a slave girl.

A slave girl quivers in the throes of uncertainty and is often found on the edge of sanity. A powerful woman finds no sanctuary there, for she knows that all of her power lies in the certainty that if she takes actions on behalf of her glorious dreams and waits patiently, she will be met with opportunity presented to her by her partner, Mother/Father God.

A slave girl sets herself up for failure with her impatience backed by fear. A powerful woman knows that fear is a poor chisel by which to carve her glorious dreams with.

To further your awakening and to power your every dream, a powerful woman knows she must often walk the seemingly hard road to forgiveness, without exception.

A slave girl refuses to give forgiveness its proper role in life.

Throughout the ages authentically powerful women and men have shown us that forgiveness is a leap toward magnificence, a return to the saintliness of oneself. You are to be reminded that One does not begin with Sainthood, but ends with it. A powerful woman knows that with each authentic step toward forgiveness progression is made in the reassembleage of HERSELF, yourself.

It is through forgiveness that you enter into a self-purified state able to hold your powerful woman steady. We tell you that it takes a fairly strenuous course of self-discipline to properly coordinate the mind, body and word to choose only the peace and power of the colossal state of forgiveness. Forgiveness only appeals to an authentically powerful woman who has no need to be right and has every desire for the bliss of internal peace. And we tell you that you were created to embody nothing less.

Too often you have been told that time takes care of the wounds that you believe were inflicted upon you that would even be the cause for forgiveness. We tell you that it is not so. Time and forgiveness have no relationship. The mind and ego are given opportunity to further their life in every single instant that you hold anger and resentment toward any person or experience.

Here is a vital key for you powerful woman. Anchor yourself firmly in the moment of Now. Have no relationship to the past and let the future unfold into what promises you fulfillment as long as you stay out of its way. Remember that the inability to forgive comes about as a result of attachments to past experience or impending future belief systems ... and they accompany a slave girls every step. Power does not exist outside the space and time of Now.

Forgive everything you think you have done wrong, forgive everything you may have indeed done without clarity, forgive everyone you are currently holding in contempt. A powerful woman does not rob themselves or another of the opportunity to become more of who they are.

Surrender your belief system that has been kept alive by your mind and ego and introduce yourself to your knowing system that lives in your heart. Here in your knowing system you will know for sure that all of humanity that has been held under the veils of forgetfulness has spent most of their human incarnation acting out of fear. Doing so has created numerous opportunities for you and your brothers and sisters to behave without consideration for Self or each other. Forgive yourself, forgive them, for under the marching orders of fear, all are subject to inconsiderate, uncompassionate behavior. No one human has escaped and no one will until all are forgiven. Start the ball rolling, powerful woman. It all begins and ends with you, whether you believe it or not.

The final stage of a fully awakened, alert, activated powerful woman comes as a result of vigilant and particular commitments that she makes with her Self daily, honoring ... above all else ... the Divinity and grandeur that resides within her, having no nostalgia for broken promises and self betrayals. Commitment to Self, Commitment to Loving Self above all else is the next and final step in the awakening of a powerful woman.

There are thirteen Commitments, the Masters number. Though many believe it to be twelve, it is not. Please take to heart the sacredness of each.

1. The first commitment is that while in the midst of fear and mental clamoring you agree to stop yourself in your tracks, take a deep, slow, quiet breath and ask your heart, your body and your soul what it needs in that given moment for *your* peace, not another's, your peace. With answer received vow to take an immediate action to accommodate them in spite of the pull from your mind or ego. This is a re-creative action and a necessary first commitment.

2. The second commitment is that you will stop struggling and desperately trying to hold on to that which was never meant for you to hold onto in the first place. In faith you commit to loosening your grip and allow for something or nothing (in the moment) to take its place. Have faith that something greater than what you struggle for will take its place, once you have made room for it.

3. The third commitment is that you will stop hoping and waiting for something in the world external to change in order for you to be happy, safe and secure. You commit to reaching deep inside of yourself to extract happiness and joy and as a result you will

come to realize that happiness, joy, safety and security is the consequence of your personal effort.

4. The fourth commitment is that you will give yourself permission to not be perfect. Perfection is a matter of mental opinion. You are making a commitment to no longer being held hostage by distorted self-judgment or the distortions of what other's opinions are of you. As long as you are actively and consciously *being* the BEST YOU CAN BE at any given moment by amplifying love, compassion, integrity, and a forgiving nature you are championing yourself to your powerful magnificent self … and that is perfect.

5. Your fifth commitment is to cease believing that you are your experiences. Remember the mind and ego are dependent and addicted to using experience as a way to define you. YOU are not your experiences, though all of your experiences have value and meaning. Your commitment is to find the heart's value and meaning in every experience. Once realized, you will have fulfilled the moment of any experience you were meant to have. And then, powerful woman, you will walk in the Light of a Truth about your experiences that are far past what the mind presently knows.

6. Your sixth commitment is to fully realize that people don't always say what they mean or mean what they say and that not everyone will always be there for you regardless of their words or promises ... and that it's not about you, ever. It's nothing personal. It's about them. So you learn to be compassionate toward yourself, and intelligent, using the wisdom of your heart in making your selection of personal companions ... and in the process irrefutable evidence of who you are rises and a realization of the importance of Self reliance is born.

7. Your seventh commitment is to fully accept and embrace your magnificent living organism that is your physical body, your temple, one of Gods many mansions. The wise One, Jesus, said this: "Your body is a tiny fence around a little part of a glorious and complete idea." When you arrive at this glorious conclusion for yourself you become obviously glorious.

8. The eighth commitment is that you will relentlessly seek contentment. The key to contentment is gratitude for what is, right now. The deepest contentment you will ever experience is when you are grateful for all

that you have, right now. Seek every opportunity to express your gratitude. This commitment is dependent upon keeping tight reins on your mind and ego. Each moment that you offer yourself contentment you are able to touch your internal Heaven and expose your powerful Divine Self.

9. The ninth commitment is that you will allow yourself, without judgment, to live on the border line between your old thinking and your new understandings of what it takes to live as a powerful woman. As you dispose of your personal criticism, you will be delivered to your compassion.

10. The tenth commitment is that you open both mind and heart to new possibilities for the new woman that has emerged in you. She has different wants and needs than the former one. With authentic and powerful self intact you will naturally begin reassessing and redefining who you are via your heart, not your mind. Stand joyfully at the threshold of your new woman and allow yourself to expand and investigate and become fascinated with the infinite possibilities that await you. This commitment will allow you to rediscover what you purposefully

stand for and once discovered you will stand up tall and strong and bold and soft.

11. The eleventh commitment is that you will no longer engage in toxic relationships of any sort, not with yourself and not with another. You, powerful woman, no longer have need of such ridiculousness. You will discover for yourself that the only relationship of any value for your life or purpose is your relationship to Love.

12. The twelfth commitment is that you will learn to live a life of integrity without compromise. Commit to knowing this Truth: You are only in integrity when the inside of yourself and the outside of yourself are in harmony. There exists no other definition. Integrity is irrevocably linked to authentic power. That truth coupled with an unwavering commitment to Love will unleash the most powerful magnificent woman you could ever imagine yourself to be.

13. And finally, powerful woman, take deeply into your heart this next commitment … a commitment held reverently and devotionally by every great and powerful Being of Light in Human form that has ever walked your Earth or is currently walking your Earth. You must establish a conscious daily rapport and

interaction with that which Created you. You will discover that by this commitment backed by your action all conceptions of limitation and lack and guilt and pain and shame and remorse will be cast away.

MEDITATION

Please use beautiful and relaxing music to bring yourself into a relaxed state. Record the words below in your own voice for this meditation if you do not have the CD. Your own words will make a strong impact on you and into you at a cellular level. Or simply read them and let them rest inside of your heart.

"From the Pure Light of God that I Am, I open to receive the Light of all that is.

I call forth the Pure White Light of Christ and I know that I am surrounded and protected as I open myself to receive my love and my power and the love and the power of the One that created me."

Take a long and steady breath. You are about to meet the Holy One that lives inside the temple of your being.

Take another long and steady breathe. Breathe in pure white light through your nose and let that Light reach and touch every corner of your being. Exhale that pure white Light, forming a circle around you with it.

Breathe in deeply, consciously again and let pure white Light touch the very center of your heart where you and God meet and touch and create together. Breathe out and let the assuredness of your breath circle you.

Breathe in Pure White Light once again and as you exhale, let the Light go as high, as wide and as deep as you can imagine it can.

In your mind's eye, while enfolded in your circle of pure White Light take yourself to the center of your heart. Notice a small chamber in your heart's center that contains within it a powerful spark of Light. That is the Light of the ONE PURE GOD that created you. That is God's outpost in you.

That is where the Source of your freedom is. This is where your powerful woman is fully awakened. There is no other place where you are to ever go again for your Source of information, or to inflame your Self-Love. This is your safe harbor.

Take another deep breath into your heart and connect to that powerful spark of Light. Exhale and feel yourself expanded. Take another deep breath and connect deeper, deeper, deeper still until you are no longer separated from that powerful spark of Light. Exhale a long steady breath and once again, allow it to circle around you.

Rest comfortably; there is a message about to be spoken to you from the Source of your Creation.

I AM here with you my child. I Am here. I Am here to help you fully awaken.

I Am here to watch over you and to love you as you fully awaken to your power and use your Divine heritage to lead by example.

Since the beginning of your Creation, I have always known you would awaken to your powerful feminine Self, because you promised that you would.

I have long known that you would keep your promise even when you went into the deepest of sleeps.

I Am here with you as you take your final breaths as sleeping beauty, and awaken to the Powerful woman that you are.

I am here to remind you of promises I made to you in exchange for the promise you made to Me.

I promised that I would never judge one moment of your journey to your awakened Self.

And I do not.

I promised that I would support your every awakened moment and I Will.

I promised that I would move Heaven closer to you upon your awakening, and it is being done in this moment.

And I promised I would come ever closer to you as you came closer to yourself, and I AM.

I Am in awe of the masterpiece I created.

I Am in awe of your beauty and your courage and your commitment and I Am honored to have a part of Me living inside of you.

Here in the center of your heart is where I have kept company with the most powerful part of yourself awaiting your arrival. Now that you have arrived, will you continue to keep company with Us?

Will you cease looking for external understanding to validate your eternal worth? Your worth never existed in the world external or through a mortal mind.

It always has and always will lie in here in the center of your heart with Me and from time to time it will be reflected back to you from the world external, but not always.

I want you to know that your very presence when fully awakened allows every other being of my Creation a greater opportunity to experience their own greatness. You have been created to make a difference in My world. And I love you.

Will you believe Me when I tell you how grateful I am that I created you exactly as you are? And will you come to peace knowing that Truth?

Do you know how much I love you?

When you forget, come to Me and I will remind you. When you remember come to Me and we will celebrate.

I will make two more promises to you and I will ask you to make two to Me.

Never forget Who You Are and I promise that I will always take care of you.

Promise to never push me away and I promise to daily show you the many ways in which I love you.

May the Light of ALL that is good and great and powerful and wise accompany you on your magnificent journey, powerful woman. I travel inside of your every footstep.

Namaste

Cosmic Wisdom

$\mathcal{M}$ ore than a dozen years ago, a being of Light calling himself Hadriel made his presence known to me while in meditation. His energy came into my home with the velocity of a thunderstorm on a calm day, yet simultaneously gave me a feeling of wellbeing and protection. At first I confused his energy with The Archangel Metatron whom I had come to know well, and who I lovingly referred to as the "blow-torch," but upon inquiry I came to know this as a different Cosmic Being of Light from whom I had requested assistance during this and one other specific lifetime.

This Being of Light called himself Hadriel.

"Why are you here?" I asked.

"I am here to remind you and escort you in the ways in which to restore your Divinity through the knowledge and wisdom that you have relentlessly pursued since you awakened. You haven't learned to trust your inner wisdom yet, but soon you will."

Rather than responding, I took a deep breath, feeling gratitude in my heart. Hadriel's parting words to me for that day were, "Prepare yourself."

It was several months before he returned.

What you are about to read are some of the answers to some of the questions that I asked Hadriel over many years about what it takes to Master the lower aspects of human consciousness, how to abolish the programmed strong hold of the mind and ego, how to effectively dissolve discordant belief systems and energetic incongruencies along with the exacting ways to use our alchemical abilities and our higher consciousness in appropriate ways.

All any one of us needs to know is how to live up to our Greater Selves during the Greater Times Ahead and then simply be.

I bring forth these answers not as a channel but as a vessel of Light in service to the all at this most critical juncture in our evolutionary history. Though it was Hadriel that inspired this discourse, throughout its evolution many of Higher Consciousness added unto it.

Please consider deeply each answer. I believe they will greatly empower you, compose and settle your soul after lifetimes of turmoil while giving you a broader perspective of Who You Really Are and What You Are Truly Capable of. You will find I didn't ask for external prophecy, I focused fully on our internal personal world. What I asked for me, I asked for you. No separation.

Over the years Hadriel and other realms of Higher Consciousness, including my own higher One, reminds me that true knowledge stems neither from the authority of others nor from a blind allegiance to antiquated dogmas. Breathe in only what resonates with your heart.

Knowledge, like Wisdom, is Light communicated to the innermost privacy of your heart through the impartial pathways of the Divine. Then, by our exacting actions do we experience Illumination and the Miracle called Life.

Question: Hadriel, what is the primary reason humans struggle to find inner peace?

Answer: It is a case of mistaken identity. Most of human nature believes they are a product of their experiences and they act and unfold their lives in accordance to that inappropriate perspective, creating ongoing struggle and strife.

Let me first give you a simplified insight into your true identity and later we will discuss experience further.

You are God. That is who you are and the only identity you can be. Each and every one of you was created from The Highest Energy of Omnipotent, Creative, Pure Love and Intelligence that exists. Many call that Omnipotent, Creative Love and Intelligence God.

Simply defined, God is The Principal consciousness and awareness that pervades all space and time. God is infinite and cannot be made known without becoming something finite. Everything finite is born of God though everything finite has a defining label for identification and experiential purposes, be it human being, angelic being, galactic being, animal, tree, rock, ocean or star. In all cases all of creation that is finite is connected irrevocably to the Infinite and to each other. All were created from One Spirit, that of God's.

Though humans have come through many wombs through numerous incarnations notice the symbology of the severing of your umbilical cord from your Earthly mothers each time you were reborn. You were meant to come through their pathways for evolution of your souls, not to be irrevocably corded to them.

The umbilical cord of your original Parent God has never been cut and can never be cut or you would cease to exist. That cord remains intact always in the center of your heart. You and God were never meant to part, ever.

You are God in finite form. And as such you are a God in partnership with the Primary God of your creation. Human beings and all things finite were created as secondary Gods in order that Primary God would have countless outlets and partners to express in a multitude of unlimited ways. In order for Primary God to experience Unlimited Potential made manifest, He and She (as One being) required a host of secondary Gods and not only in human form.

It is the human form, however, through which God has the greatest opportunities to have a multitude and a plentitude of diverse expressions.

The identification problem arose when the human being who agreed to fall under the veils of forgetfulness for a period of time began using their experiences as a means of identification and validation or invalidation.

Further complicating matters, human beings turned to their minds and to others who *appeared* to be the only avenue for answers for who they were and what their experiences meant in relationship to definition of Self.

Armed with inaccurate perceptions and assumptions human beings began the decline of who they truly were and began the process of making themselves up as they collected and installed erroneous belief systems about themselves and each other.

Mortal Consciousness gained momentum eventually edging Divine consciousness out. Thus, the problems of both internal unrest and external unrest began. One simply mirrored the distortions of the other.

What humans are now calling the Ascension would more accurately be called the Rebirth of God

Consciousness. This rebirth is being propagated by the Divine heart and soul of every human.

Both your Hearts and Souls are each demanding a halt to mistaken identities and a return to Pure God Consciousness. Your hearts and souls have carried the burden of having an inappropriate and inaccurate experience to Life long enough and are no longer willing to yield to the personality, ego or Mortal mind. Your heart and soul have never lost their true identity and are craving relief.

Key to true evaluation of Self and retrieved identity is the realization that experiences are not defining moments, they are simply opportunities to either come back to the heart of who each of you are or opportunities that allow the Truth of who you are to show up in tangible form.

You are Gods in finite form, for a period of time until you return and merge with the Infinite Gods that you are. You are each an outpost of the Divine, of God. We in the Higher Realms know who you are and love you as the Gods that you are.

As you turn the page in your evolutionary history you are all being asked to embrace that truth, and act in accordance with that truth.

Question: Hadriel, are we somehow to be blamed because we forgot and turned to experience for our definition?

Answer: There is no blame here, simply awareness and the time for reconciliation with the Truth. Humans have allowed themselves to be overthrown time and again by the masterful manipulations of a mind that goes to extremes to keep them from their true identity.

Experience is the most effective way for mortal mind to operate and foster separation from God Consciousness because experience leaves an impression in the human mind to interpret its meaning.

It is impossible for the human mind to have a true relationship with experience, for it is limited in its perceptions of meaning and outcomes and more often than not believes it knows everything about any experience it has.

Take note for yourself of the ways in which your mind provides you rationale, reasons, pros and cons for anything and everything. Note how it repeats to you, the catcher of the information, the same material over and again regardless of the experience or circumstance. Mortal mind uses only what has been formerly programmed into as a means to an end whether now or later.

Long after an experience is over the Mortal mind is still having it, interpreting it, and creating further aspects of it that are not only far from the truth of their meaning but interrupts the possibilities that lie within the experience to advance toward the Mind of God.

Again I say without judgment or blame the Mortal Mind is incapable of having a pure and spontaneous experience with experience. It is only when tapping into the Immortal Mind or mind of God while in between thoughts that right relationship to experience can be had.

If each one of you will simply remember that Life is a creative idea that can only find itself in changing forms, attachment and identification to any single experience will be easier let go of once the blessing of it has been received.

Question: Hadriel, you talk about God Consciousness vs. Human or Mortal Mind Consciousness. What exactly is consciousness and what is the difference between the two?

Answer: Consciousness is the presence of your Being. It is the source of impulse, drive, desire, and emotional energy. It is Self-awareness and inner sensibility. Consciousness is the vehicle for inter-dimensional communication and multidimensional integration, both essential for enlightenment and evolution.

Human Consciousness is one that is distracted and enmeshed by circumstances of the outer world, rarely allowing one pure presence and connection to your higher self, to others, or to Primary God Consciousness.

Human consciousness or lower consciousness takes external life personally, distorting the truth of who you are. Human consciousness has a propensity to lean toward the drama of day-to-day activities (or distortions), which the human race believes to be life.

Personal emotional need and the grasping for things and people in the world external has eclipsed deep spiritual need, lowering human consciousness.

Higher consciousness or God Consciousness is your finite being of Creation filled with creative impulse, joy, love, compassion, wisdom and truth. It is you, individuated human, awakened to your Divine nature, in spite of the human one present.

One of higher consciousness is one who is fully connected to only what is present in the moment, having no relationship to time patterns of past or future. It is not void of feeling, though it is independent of mental and emotional reactions.

One of higher consciousness is mentally quiet, yet completely aware, witnessing circumstances and experiences, allowing them to be as they are, extracting the nectar from them and then watching them pass.

A higher consciousness or God Consciousness allows an organic conclusion, rather than a contrived, personally involved one, to arise.

Humanity is poised for re-birthing of God Consciousness on your Planet of Earth. It has reached its lowest point of density and its maximum amount of separation from the purest essence of Love and Light.

Perhaps more than at any other time in your personal evolution, you are each being given much Universal and multi-dimensional love and support, though at times it may feel otherwise, it is not so.

For this re-birthing to be accomplished each of you must have a deep and abiding personal devotion to re-establishing God Consciousness which includes a mind void of lack and limitation, a fully opened heart, and exacting actions devoted to raising your consciousness daily.

Question: What are exacting actions and how do we know we are taking the right one?

Answer: The "exacting action" being called for now requires your own discernment as to the actions that are most appropriate for your LIFE to spiral upward to meet the passions of your soul. Exacting actions do not require money, though many believe it does, it does not. All that is required is intention and action backed by love and courage. It is a short recipe that will feed you for a lifetime.

Question: Hadriel, what happens to those who stop short of making that commitment to rise up to God Consciousness or their fullest potential?

Answer: The rebirthing of Consciousness for each individual is the only way that will give any one of you a way to end the *life* of your circumstances.

Each of you must be able to function from a higher perspective of yourself and create more life from there or you will noticeably fall from Grace. One who chooses to stop short of their full potentials will find no means of

Universal Cosmic Support. The reason being that Primary God, the very soul of who you are, no longer desires the experience of further decline, nor does your Planet of Earth.

Like you, your Earth is a finite being of Primary God. She is living consciousness and the embodiment of Primary Creator Source. Like you, she was created as an outlet and a partner to express God in a multitude of ways as well as to be the foundation upon which humanity and nature could express, naturally.

Your earth has reached her maximum capacity of enduring negative unconscious energy penetrating and disrupting her natural balance, as have you. Your Earth, like you, has been affected and infected deeply by humanities turmoil and fear.

Earth's full potential to reside peacefully with you and all of Creation has been greatly impeded. You each witness and are subject to her now frequent violent reactions and throwing off of the excessive negative energy that has invaded her. Do you not do the same? You see one aspect of Creation greatly affects all aspects of Creation.

Maintaining a lower frequency of consciousness will continue to create suffering inside the temple of your beings rendering you incapable of internal peace. That is the answer to your question. Still, you are each at choice as to which consciousness you will allow to inhabit you. Fortunately or unfortunately the fight for your life is either won or lost in the battlefield of the human mind.

If you each pay close attention you will notice that not a single experience will come your way any longer that will not be prompting you to choose a higher or lower consciousness while in the midst of it. I offer you this.

In the midst of any experience you are having, put a net around every faithless and discordant thought you are having about it. Toss it into the vastness of the Universe for transmutation. State aloud your intention of severing your connection with it. Hold that intention, do not touch it with another thought and then watch it disappear.

When you have effectively done so, go within to the quiet place in your heart and simply ask this question: "What do I need to know about this experience that will bring forth wisdom and lift my consciousness?" Sit still, be patient and the lamp of Truth will be turned on.

Question: Why do humans make choices that ultimately work against themselves?

Answer: Primarily as a result of lack of clarity coupled with the promptings of fear over love. Wherever there is fear, clarity is not.

Most of humanity rushes to their decisions through a split second reaction caused by a charge, be it high or low, to the emotional body and mind. The human race is largely a fast-paced society running on adrenaline and reaction far more often than clarity.

When it comes to choices, the Mortal Mind and human ego (which is actually an illusion more wisely saved for another conversation) immediately perk up, ready for action. Both, with their illusory natures, impede upon your consciousness to steer you in one way or another based on *their* perceived need, whether now or in the future.

What you may not realize is that whenever a choice arises, both your God Consciousness and your human consciousness speak to you and vie for your attention.

How often have you said aloud or silently, "Part of me wants this, and part of me wants that?" The parts of yourself you are referring to are mind and ego, or heart and soul. Both speak to you when a choice is at hand.

The part that wins your affection will either be your mind and ego, or your heart and soul.

When a human being consorts with their Mortal mind regarding choice one is kept hostage to choices based on fixed notions, other people's opinions, or the promise of external fulfillment. If this is the place from which you choose pay close attention and you will notice yourself being dragged into former impulses based on fear of the future or external ambition....always.

When you make your choice from the impulse being given to you from your heart and soul, though you may be temporarily afraid, you are being steered toward clarity. The heart and soul hold only love for you and are turning you in the direction that is noble and holds the greatest promise for you.

No doubt if any of you look back upon your lives you will notice how operating without clarity weakened you in various ways. Lack of clarity sets up a bounty of circumstances requiring you to expend enormous amounts of energy and often times resources to find your way out of.

Before we close this particular point of conversation it's important to be aware of this fact. You live on a Planet with a mass consciousness whose every thought vibrates out into your fields of energy every single second of every single day, often attaching themselves to you and filtering into your own personal thought systems.

In part, that is another reason why many are often confused and thrown out of clarity. Imagine thousands and thousands of thoughts daily being hurled at you through the ethers and often disguising themselves as if they were your own. They are not. This is where singular discernment while in a state of stillness would greatly serve you. It will open a space for your heart and soul to speak to you and offer clarity.

Remember your clarity cannot come through another. It can only come through your soul, your Higher Self or strong connection with God Consciousness. Many of your guides are also unable to bring you clarity, for they are with you to support your personal breakthrough into God Consciousness, and often remain silent as a means of support.

Because Clarity is one of the greatest gifts you can give unto yourselves to merge with God Consciousness, or your higher selves, let me share with you five exacting pieces of wisdom that will direct you into the light of clarity.

First: Create a quiet and sacred place for yourself without any form of distraction.

Second: Always begin by breathing. Breathe as long as you must to calm your nervous system and to move in the opposite direction of your mind into the portal of your heart. Take a minimum of three deep and steady breaths in, allowing your breath to reach all of the edges of your being and connect you with God Consciousness. Exhale with awareness.

Third: Identify specifically what you are in need of clarity about. It is vital for you to be specific. Gaining clarity must be specifically about you, not someone else. This exacting action is not for you to gain someone else's clarity, it is for your clarity whether it involves another or not.

At this point I suggest that you are prepared to write down whatever you desire to be clear about (or have clarity about) as well as speaking it out loud to the inner reaches of your soul and the outermost reaches of Universe.

Fourth: call forth patience, stillness of thoughts, and control of your breath to allow the request to be set forth, heard and responded to. You would be wise to make a promise to yourself at this point that your clarity will be gotten from your world internal, rather than anyone in the external world.

And finally: detach from the outcome and from time. Time has no relationship to clarity. Furthermore you are asking for clarity, not information for your mind and ego to barter with. Be patient and you will gain clarity. Remember, Divine Timing is involved with your clarity. Be patient and be still.

When you gain clarity it may not be what your mind or ego thought, or what the *lower I* thought it needed. Rest comfortably in the knowing that clarity comes to you from the God Consciousness that resides within you. Clarity about anything travels into your consciousness via the route of silence.

Question: Hadriel, what do humans fear most and how do we rise above that which we fear the most?

Answer: Human beings fear being out of control of outcomes in their own personal lives. They fear the state of mystery. That state of fear perpetuates continual thinking into the mind that sets that fear in motion to begin with, restless watching and skittish maneuvering to attempt to gain an immediate answer to that which they think they need. Those actions never allow an absolute relationship to life to unfold naturally, or the path of mystery to spiral One upward leaving the mundane and predictable behind.

Do not misunderstand this to mean that you are not meant to participate in the creation of your life and experiences, it means for enlightenment to occur in your life your participation includes participating with the unknown, peacefully. It means realizing that the uncreated parts of your life are part of your unfolding Creation.

As long as human beings keep themselves in a constant state of perpetual motion attempting to control their lives coupled with endless striving, and grasping internal peace will remain a constant desire, rather than a state of being. Mystery is a great part of what composes God Consciousness.

Because mystery is neither apparent to your senses nor obvious to your intellect, many find it unnerving and adopt a belief that their life is out of control. It is not.

Mystery is the fantastical journey into the realm of potential that makes boundaries dissolve and minds expand.

No part of creation was created to know everything. You took on your human form to have an adventure that would heal parts of your soul and, en route, to return you to your true identity — Love in form, God in form. This can only be accomplished in the ocean of mystery. Without embracing mystery, a human being cannot build trust, true courage cannot exist, and faith has no point of entry.

Without mystery human life spins out of control as it is taken over by the Mortal mind that has no relationship to Infinite Possibility. So why fear that which offers such freedom?

Mystery is uncertainty, not lack of clarity. It is the place where all Masters place themselves to experience unlimited outcomes, unlimited potentials, unlimited grace.

I remind you once again that when the human mind encounters uncertainty, it rapidly seeks an answer through its limited comprehension and evaluation system. It selects its answer from a small box of potential answers and believes it has resolved something. The mind believes then that it has effectively controlled uncertainty and, through the natural course of life, moves on to the next uncertainty.

This sets up an ongoing matrix of *limited* individual control.

Life lived gracefully within the scope of mystery or uncertainty is life expanded and opened to its fullest potential, allowing the grace and majesty of God to enter with myriad possibilities. If humans realized how much they have limited themselves by seeking to escape uncertainty, they would be dismayed at what could have been.

Mystery shapes itself without human mind control, and given the chance frees every one of you from survivalist mentality. When you are no longer tethered to survival, you will feel the bliss of freedom and you will never again consent to trying to control your every turn. When you dance with mystery, you dance with Creation.

Your greatest poets, artists, and writers emerged from the house of mystery. Every saint, sage, and mystic lived in the house of mystery, and they came to know their relationship to life because of it.

Mystery is not meant to be a setup for human fear; it is simply life not divulging all of its plans at once. It is a way to keep you present in the moment that *is*, while experiences and circumstances are being created for your life. Whenever mystery appears before you, God Consciousness is in it asking you to surrender the outcome.

Mystery is a Divine part of life, and none of human nature are meant to fall in its sudden breeze. Learn to live in the mystery of Life, and enjoy it, rather than being tormented by it. Do you think that the Creator of all is not in a constant state of Mystery? Remember you were created in his and her likeness.

Question: Hadriel, it seems a bit arrogant to walk around calling ourselves God.

Answer: If you were not God you would cease to exist, as we spoke about earlier. You are an imposter if you claim yourself to be anything else.

In great part humans are God's biggest challenge in your time now, because so many refuse to identify themselves properly and to express themselves properly. Instead, far too many of you continue to make an unconscious pact with fear based human behavior and carry on *with* it as if it were your Gods.

Again I say, You are God and you actually proclaim it every time you utter the words I Am That I Am, which many of you do. You make the proclamation that you are God, though refuse to live what you speak.

Look at yourselves in the mirror each day. Speak the words aloud I Am That I Am as you look directly into your eyes, the window to your soul. You will see the God that lives inside of you shining through you each time you proclaim your identity. You can never proclaim it enough. Every cell in your body surges with new life as you open yourself to the Truth.

Once your deep understanding of the fact that you are God turns into remembering, and remembering becomes knowing, and knowing becomes being what you know, your consciousness is going to rise so high that you will never fasten yourself to a false identity again. You will not choose the maintenance of a false identity when you come to know the wisdom and truth of I Am that I Am.

Once you claim and express from your original identity of Gods in form you will be taken outside the time and space of your narrow personal lives, and be connected with your Infinite and eternal lives.

It would be wise for each of you to, once and for all, be done with the parts of yourself that cause you to suffer. Fuse yourselves with the Mind and Heart of God and then you will know the inherent wisdom of the ages and fully live your miraculous lives.

You, the chosen modern day disciples of the Holiest of Holies, are coming closer each day to your true identity. Some of you are being forced toward it while others are leaping into it. It is all of Creation's greatest desire that you each heed the Clarion call of your hearts and Souls. Bless and acknowledge the ending of a time in your evolution that no longer serves. Claim your true identity and know you are deeply loved.

Namaste

The Five Contemplations Of Bliss
Balance, Love, Integrity, Sexuality, Soul

*W*ith any of these contemplations, if you don't also have the CD, (available at www.maureenmoss.com) you may choose to read them as affirming contemplations, or record them with your own words. Choose background music that soothes your soul when you listen. Make each one count!

Balance

If you are reading the contemplations, please read them slowly. Consider contemplating one each day. If you prefer to continue to read them one after the other, please make a decision to sincerely take them into your heart, so they are able to make a difference in shifting your present consciousness.

Please take three steady, slow intentional breaths in and out, (pause) in and out, (pause) in and out. Please do that three times, consciously, slowly, and lovingly.

Imagine that you are sitting by the ocean, watching the waves as they flow in and flow out. Feel the heat of the sand beneath you. Feel the warming rays of the sun as they embrace and bless you. Hear the sea gulls as they cry out in joy at this wonder of this day. They are lifted by the gentle breeze off the ocean, and this breeze comes to you full of the smell of salt, full of freshness as it brushes your cheeks. Now the breeze begins to blow through your mind and clear it completely of all thought. The breeze is clearing every thought from your mind, blowing gently through, leaving you calm and refreshed, open and calm and ready to be, simply be, on this perfect day.

Watch the waves flowing in and flowing out, looking deeply into one of the waves, so deeply that you feel yourself becoming the wave, and then find that you are merged with the ocean itself. You are one with it completely. You have no thoughts, for the ocean does not think. It simply is. It does not wish, plan or worry. It simply is, in a deep and powerful peace. It has its tides, it has its movements, up and down, but through it all, it simply is.

Feel yourself as one with the ocean, with the peace and deep wisdom of the ocean. You are as deeply wise as this ocean, this ocean which endures and moves and is, deeply in peace.

Nothing disrupts the heart of the ocean. Storms may come and go, tides may move, fish may swim through, but nothing disrupts the peace and flow within the ocean itself. And you are this as well. You are this ocean, calm and peaceful and simply being. Letting life move through you and over you, under you and around you. And you simply are. You are the ocean and you are at peace.

Take a pause and breathe.

And in the deep wisdom of the ocean, you know that you can let your life be like this. No matter what happens, you can breathe deeply and be the ocean. You can let your emotions come and go like the tide, yet not let them throw you off balance. You can learn to let them pass through and by, you can learn to let them be, one experience after another, one emotion after another, as waves upon the beach, coming in and going out, beginning and completing, flowing one after the other, each coming into being and then passing out of being and back into the peace and wisdom which is the ocean.

For you know life is like this, that what comes in passes out, what flows up onto the beach, returns again back into the whole. Experiences are like this, they come and go and flow. And yet you are not this wave lapping on the beach. You are not this experience or that. You are the ocean, whole and complete, and what moves through you and on your edges, does not define you. You are the ocean and you are whole and complete and at peace, no matter what happens outside you, no matter what moves through you.

You do not judge what happens. The ocean does not judge. You do not fear what might come. The ocean has no fear. What is, is. What flows, flows. You allow it all to be, allowing things to begin and end and complete their flow, without thinking them good or bad, without thinking yourself good or bad. They simply are. You simply are. And all is whole and complete in the flow of the ocean, the ocean which is you, and the ocean which is life, for you are life, you are connected to all that is, you are one with all that is, in this great ocean which is life, which is you. You are one with all, and it flows.

And for a moment, just feel this. Feel your peace. Feel your wholeness, your completeness, your oneness with all that is, in peace. Feel how you are everything you need to be, right now.

Take a pause and breathe.

For just a moment, think of something that has been bothering you, something that has been on your mind. Perhaps it is a worry, a hurt, a betrayal, a thought or an emotion which has troubled you and disturbed your peace, something your mind does not want to let go of. For just a moment, bring it before you.

Feel this thought, this emotion, this so-called problem, feel it just move through you, wash over you and dissipate into the sea, the sea which is you. Feel how it is nothing compared to your great and abiding presence and peace. Feel how it is small and transient, a little drop of water that comes and goes. But you, you are the ocean, deep and wise and eternal. Feel how little problems are nothing to you, they are just waves, the little peaks and valleys of life, but you are deep, deep and peaceful and undisturbed. You are life itself. You are the ocean.

Take a pause and breathe.

Suggestion: Today, as you go through your day, keep coming back to this ocean of peace. When you are tense, take a deep breath. Hear the ocean as it crashes on the waves. Hear the seagulls calling. Be one with the ocean. Be at peace.

If you begin to judge or criticize yourself or anyone else, notice the wave of judgment and then release it, release it to flow back into the ocean, the ocean which accepts all in her great wisdom and peace.

When you are in pain, know that this is an experience that will pass, as all experiences do not attempt to hold onto it. It is a wave which is pushing its way up onto the sand, but it will recede. Just allow it to flow as it needs to flow, allow it to pass through you, and know that it will return to the great ocean of you, making your life fuller for the experience, the experience of life, the pleasures and pains, the things which are and come and go, in fullness and being, a part of the ocean, a part of life.

Do not fight against the tides or the current. Do not try to hold on to the waves as they pass. Do not try to control the natural ebb and flow of life. Just be. Just be and know that you are all that you need to be for the life which is flowing toward you today. You are enough. You are the ocean.

As you go out into the world today, remember that you are the ocean. Remember to let the experiences flow easily over you and through you. Remember to just be, deeply in peace and within wisdom. Be the ocean you are.

Love

Please take three steady, slow intentional breaths in and out, (pause) in and out, (pause) in and out. Please do that three times, consciously, slowly, and lovingly. Prepare yourself as you did for the contemplation of *Balance.*

Come with me now, deep, deep into the heart of the world, where flows an endless river. It is a river of love, and all that exists is sustained by this river, comes from this river, and is the river itself.

And see now that you are a tree, a tree with roots that reach down through the soil of this life and into the waters of endless love. Your roots reach down and pull this love into your life, where it sweetens all that is and makes you blossom all over with love.

Yes, you are a tree and the river of love runs deep in your trunk, filling you and making you strong. It fills your heart of love with love for yourself, endless love, a deep love, for you know that you are also made of the river, and loving yourself is as natural and easy as being, for you are a part of the river which flows endlessly, you are a part of all that is, connected to all that is. And so the most natural and easy thing you can possibly do is allow yourself to love yourself, exactly as you are, without criticism, without striving and trying, just being, being who you are, a part of the endless flow of love.

Your trunk, your center, your heart of love, grows stronger and stronger the more you drink and fill yourself with love. And as you do this, you begin to send out branches, branches that reach up into the sky, as you express yourself and all the love you are. And out upon these branches, begin to form little buds, promising buds, buds which want to open and send their perfume out into the world.

These flowers are there to perfume the world with your presence, but they draw their sustenance from the trunk, which is full of love. And if you do not love yourself, if you do not learn to fill yourself with this love of self and this love of life itself, then you will not have the power and strength to blossom forth with all of the love which will help others as well as yourself.

Take a pause and breathe.

Of these blossoms, the first is compassion. With compassion you express your love by paying attention to others, by noticing their pain, their fears, and their joy. See them as they are and accept them, just as they are. They are a reflection of you, dear One. As such, this reflection of you stems from your acceptance of yourself, for when you accept yourself completely, no matter how you are, no matter what you do or is done to you, then it is a natural and easy thing to accept others as they are, to give them the freedom to be themselves, just as you give it to yourself, and to allow everyone to blossom forth in their own way and in their own time.

The flower of compassion does not know judgment or criticism. The flower of compassion is deeply connected and knows that each person is a treasure, each has ways to blossom forth, and if we can point another in the direction of love, if we can help them direct their own roots down into the endless river of love, all can blossom, all can bloom. And sometimes compassion is as simple as this, to point the way. And sometimes it is a good deal more, to spend time and caring for another, to share your light and love with them, so that they may better find their own peace inside.

Now, just for just a moment, fill yourself with love, pull it into your trunk and let it fill you. And then, let the blossom of compassion spring out on your branches. Think of someone you know who has seen some trouble, someone of whom you have been judgmental or critical, and give them the gift of acceptance and caring. Give them a flower of compassion.

Take a pause and breathe.

And now, think of times you have judged yourself. Think of criticism you have laid upon yourself. And extend to yourself this same acceptance. Extend to yourself this same love. Accept yourself exactly as you are. Give yourself a flower of compassion.

As your love for yourself deepens, as you are able to fill yourself with love instead of criticism and judgment, you will find that you want to give, you want to give just because there are things which need to be done and you are someone who just might be able to do them. You will find, as you love yourself more and more, that you have many impulses to do things for other people.

At first, you may not wish to act on these impulses due to former fears. Move past your resistance by loving yourself so much that you will not resist anything that moves your heart. Your fear of inadequacy and rejection, your fear that your life will be compromised in some way if you allow other people in, your fear that you will lose your center if you give too much to others, this will all fight against your natural desire to be of service, to help others on their path, and to help yourself. Surrender all resistance. Surrender all fear. Fill yourself with love.

The more love you give yourself, the more this fear and resistance will begin to wither away, for the more you love yourself, the more you will recognize your own power and know that, in fact, you are more than capable of helping others. The more you fill yourself with love, the less needy you will feel and the more you will realize that you do have enough to spare and share, for your roots are dipped into the endless river of love, and you have strength and power beyond imagining.

Pause and take a breath.

And so then do the flowers of selfless giving and of generosity blossom. The flower of selfless giving may require great care and preparation, and a deep commitment, a commitment to right a wrong, to end a cycle, to help turn around something which has been traveling too long in the wrong direction. It may be a commitment to a project or a group of people or a realization that miracles happen when strengths are joined together. And you are a part of this miracle, when you blossom forth in selfless giving.

The flower of generosity, though springing from the same place, is of the sudden impulse, unplanned and spontaneous. The flower of generosity may be a simple act, opening a door, picking up an item dropped, freely giving a smile, offering a seat, patiently listening to a long tale. The flower of generosity can be expressed in every moment, whenever there is someone there to receive it. It takes nothing but remembering that you can give a gift to each person you encounter, and that it will gladden both of your hearts as you do so. It is a way of thinking and being, a flower of constant awareness, a new way of life. A way of expressing love at every turn.

When these flowers are blossoming forth, when the flowers of compassion, selfless giving and generosity are in full bloom, the last flower cannot help but bloom. For this is the flower of joy, and the more the other flowers bloom, the more joy blooms as well. For joy is a flowering of self love, of love of life and of love of others. It is something you have as well as give, and the more you give it, the more you have it. For every gift of love or joy which is given, ten more blossoms spring up in its place, and the cycle is never-ending, never-ending love.

Joy is your natural state when you are living in love, giving in love. Joy is the natural expression of a life balanced in peace and flowing with love.

Pause and take a breath.

As the joy fills you, and as you give more joy to others, the roots grow stronger and even more love is pulled up from the river of love. And on and on it flows and goes, as you grow stronger, pulling in love and giving it away. And the more you give, the more you blossom and the more there is for others and the more there is for you.

For it is all one, and it is all love. For you are the river and the sky, the tree and the blossoms. And you bloom and grow, grow stronger and more magnificent with each drop of love you pull into yourself, each flower of love which blooms forth from you. And your glory grows as you cover yourself with more and more acts of love, more and more feelings of love, becoming an ever more full manifestation of the love which is you.

Take a pause and breathe.

As you go out into the world today, remember that you are love. Reach down with your roots to the unending river of love, drink deeply, blossom forth and perfume the world with love.

Integrity and Intention

Take three steady, slow intentional breaths in and out, in and out, in and out. Please do that three times, consciously, slowly, and lovingly. Prepare yourself as you did with *Balance*, and *Love*.

Let us begin with a meditation to bring you into full awareness of yourself and your connection to all that is. Be one with these words:

Dear God, I turn away from the noise of the world around me to the world of silence that lies within me. I breathe the breath that my heart would have me breathe. I breathe the breath that activates the original blueprint of my soul. I shut out all memories that are linked to the past. I create no images of the future. I focus on what my life is telling me now.

In this space, I am aware that Who I Am is a part of All That Is, and in that I find my repose. I connect my spirit to the consciousness of the one Divine Spirit – God. In this consciousness, I am aware that there is only one heart beating, the heart of all life, and I am an important beat in this Divine heart.

I am not, nor ever will be, a victim of circumstance, for that is the role of the mind. The pure intentions of my heart are always made manifest through my unwavering faith in Divine Spirit. I surrender my ego, all doubts, all worries, all fear, all anger and bask in the light of courage, faith, trust and surrender.

From that place, I become pure love, fused with the Great Universal Love, for there is only one of us. As I bring forth my love for myself, I cannot help but feel loved, for all things are one. I perceive the magnificence of Who I am and commit to assisting others in seeing their magnificence. I express my life in laughter and joy, in integrity, and in service. I add upon myself only the good, the great, the constructive, the whole, and the holiness. Nothing else is allowed into my Divine blueprint, and I am grateful to know where to find myself.

And now, for a moment, just feel this oneness with yourself, this true knowledge of yourself. Let the integrity of who you truly are fill your body and clear your mind.

Take a pause and breathe.

Out of this deep knowledge of yourself, and this deep and complete connection through love, let an intention form. Allow yourself to know and feel and understand what it is that you are here to do. Let it be a full expression of all that you are, so that what you feel, what you say and what you do are all one, are all springing from the same deep knowledge of yourself, the connection with the one that is all, and the love which flows through you and all that is. Let yourself see and feel and know what you truly intend with your life.

Take a pause and three steady breaths in and out, slowly, fully, lovingly and with your full heart. Open yourself to receive an angel.

And now an angel hovers before you. She is here to receive your intention, your desire to create your life in a way which truly expresses all that you are. She holds out a crystal heart and asks you to put your intention within it. Now allow a rainbow of love to flow from your heart into the crystal heart which rests in her hands. Let the flow be one of pure love, love for yourself in your role here in this life, love for your deepest self as you abide eternally, love for all that is. Allow this intention, filled with your deep truth and your deepest integrity, flow from your own heart into the crystal heart held by the angel. Feel it as it leaves you. Feel that you are surrendering this intention to the universe, to God, for its fullest expression to come to you as it will. Feel that you are releasing it completely. You will not try to control. You will not doubt its fulfillment. You will simply wait patiently and with wonder to see how it will be fulfilled in your life.

You will prepare yourself for the tests and challenges which will accompany it. You will prepare yourself to show courage. You will prepare yourself, most of all, to remain true to yourself even as these challenges appear. You will remain true to who you are with courage and with integrity, as the universe responds to your loving intention and moves the stars about, blows the winds and shakes the trees of life, in order that your intention may be fulfilled in love and truth.

Now the angel takes this crystal heart and flies into the heavens, where she releases your intention into the universe. See it flow out of the crystal and spread across the sky, a rainbow of loving intention. And you must release it in your heart and surrender to how it will return to you. Know that the universe will not deliver in ways you would predict. Know that it will be a great and mysterious surprise each day. Know that you will be asked to listen to guidance and to follow it in faith, faith that the universe knows best how to fulfill this intention.

Take a pause and breathe.

Now that you have reached yourself, and sent your loving and true intention out into the universe, take the following prayer, to heart. Be one with these words and love yourself. Love your God Self.

Dear God, Thank you for every blessing and for every awareness that has been brought to my life. Thank you for each moment of the day that lies before me, allowing me to create my greatest expression of love. Thank you for the opportunity to see familiar, loving faces today, that I may express my love and gratitude to them. Thank you for new and unfamiliar people and opportunities that may appear today, bringing me greater insight into myself.

May this day bring forth a freedom in my soul that I did not know yesterday. May this day remind me to be strong and compassionate. May this day show me my own courage. I ask for the outpouring of your love on every creature large and small that lives upon the back of Mother Earth. Please open my own heart even further that I may be an expression of the outpouring of Your love to all humankind. May Your light be the Light in me and may it shine undeniably wherever I am today. I thank you from my heart.

Take a pause and a breath.

As you go out into the world today, surrender to your true self. Have the courage to be fully yourself, expressing who you are in everything you say and do. Allow your highest intention to unfold in your life.

Sexuality and Sensuality

Take three steady, slow intentional breaths in and out, in and out, in and out. Please do that three times, consciously, slowly, and lovingly. Prepare yourself as you did for *Balance, Love,* and *Integrity.*

All love begins with a deep love for yourself. This includes a deep love for your body, just as it is, right now, at this age, at this weight, exactly as you are.

Begin by releasing shame and guilt, releasing all that happened to you in the past, your childhood, and the relationships you have had since then. Release it all. Release also any shame you feel about your body as it is now and any guilt you feel about living your life as you have.

Release all of that and come into now and, filled with a deep love, filled with forgiveness for all that was done to you and all that you have done and left undone in your life.

Take a pause and three steady breaths in and out, slowly, fully, lovingly and with your full heart. Open yourself to receive an angel.

See an angel hovering before you. She holds a net woven of gold, a big net to catch from you all of the things which have led you to feel shame and guilt. Her golden net will capture them and take them away from you. It will expand to hold even the biggest things, even the most frightening, things you have not wanted to think about for fear that they would overpower you. Her golden net is large enough to handle all of them. For they are large only when they are inside you. They are dark and large only when they are hidden in the dark recesses of your psyche. When you pull them out into the light of day, when you put them into the net of the angel, they will shrink down into nothingness and free you from the hold they have over you now.

Notice as she takes all of the pain and all of the hurt from you. Give it up. She will take all of the shame you have associated with this pain and hurt. She will take all of the fear that you are not enough, that you are inadequate, that you are somehow to blame for all that has happened to you. She will take it all from you. Give it to her.

Allow yourself to remove shame and guilt from yourself. Allow yourself to pull out the things you are ashamed of, from the past, from old childhood wounds, from pain of old relationships, and from how you feel about yourself now. Let them all go, release them. Dig down deep, and if you find a few more old shames, some old guilt, some blame and anger, pull it all out now and give it to the angel.

Pull it all out and put it into the golden net which the angel holds out before you now.

Take a pause and breathe.

Watch the angel fly up to the heavens, her net full of the things you have released. And there, she holds the golden net up to the light and all of the old hurts and pains, all of the blame, all of the pain and shame and guilt, transform into love, forgiving love, pure love.

Yes, sweet love, pouring love, the love of the universe, all for you And the golden clouds of light which are above you now begin to rain gently, and golden drops of love pour down upon you. They flow into your heart, filling the space where the pain and the shame once lived. They flow down upon you and cover your entire body with love, sweet love, healing love. This love is the love of self, the love of your spirit and your body both. And the love heals all. It washes clean the shame and the guilt, the anger and the blame; it removes all the pain as it covers you, washes it clean and bathes you in a gentle, sweet and golden love. You are covered with this grace, with this love and it heals you. It heals you completely. This love from the heavens, which was your pain, now turned into love, sweet love, unending love.

Take a pause and breathe.

Notice that you are full of love, pure love, forgiving love. All of the shame is gone. All of the pain is gone. All of the guilt is gone. Let it be gone. Feel yourself as love, know yourself as love.

Take another pause. And take three slow and steady breaths in and out. Loving yourself with every in breath.

We will now move down through your body, clearing and activating your energy centers, the places where the energy in your body flows in and out. We will open up the flow of energy in each center and open you to the flow of love and energy within you and without you.

Let us begin at the crown of your head. Feel yourself opening to the flow at the very top of your head. Feel the golden love of God flowing in through your head and flowing down through your body. Feel how it is all one, how the love of God and the love of this physical body are all one, for this body is the expression of God in life, for you are the expression of God in life, and your body is one with all that is. Let this flow of spirit enter you and flow down into you. Let it reach to every part of your body, filling you with the presence of God, made manifest as you.

For a moment, just feel yourself as being completely full of the grace which flows into you at the crown of your head.

Take a pause and take a breath.

Now move your attention down to the place in the middle of your forehead known as the third eye. Let the energy here open and flow, open up to the vision of who you truly are. Let the golden stream of love pour in and then see yourself through this eye of love. See yourself in your beauty, in your glory, the pure expression of your truth and your light, made manifest in this physical form. See all of this beauty and know it as you.

Take a pause and take a breath.

Allow your attention to move down to your throat, to the seat of self-expression. Let the golden love cover your throat and know that you can express who you are with honesty and integrity, making all that you say and express, all that you do and are, be in tune with the glory that is you, with the love which flows through you, with all that you are. Open up your throat so that you may sing your song, so that you sing it with your body as well as your soul, letting each action be a loving expression of self.

Take a pause and take a breath.

Please move your attention down to your heart and let the love flow. Feel how the shame and guilt are now gone, taken away by the angel. Feel how the pain is all gone, transformed now into love. Feel how the golden love from heaven has filled you to the top with love, a deep love of yourself, a forgiving love, a love which takes away the blame and anger, the regret and the fear. Feel how you can now love yourself deeply, you, just you, exactly as you are. Just as you are right now, is how you should be. Feel this. Know this. You are love.

Take a pause and breathe.

Move your focus down to your center, your solar plexus.

This is the seat of your truth. And your truth is love. And your truth is beauty, for who you are, who you truly are, is deeply beautiful. And your center, your solar plexus, is a seat of calm and goodness, residing deep within you. Feel how you have a deep pool of peace within you, right here in your center. Let the rain of golden love pool up within your center. Let it build up a deep pool of peace from which you can draw, always and ever. Let that peace fill you and make you fully aware of your own goodness. You are love. You are beauty and you are love. Feel this.

Take a pause and breathe.

Let your focus move down to your center of sexuality and sensuality. Focus your attention gently and with love. Know your sexuality, this seat of creativity and wonder, this seat of beauty and purity, as a great gift. Know this place in your body as a place of nourishment, a place where the physical blends with the spiritual to create life, to hold pure love. Know that you can learn to love this part of yourself as well. Know that this is a part of your physical body that is good, that is pure, that reaches up into spirit as surely as does every other part of your body. Know that there is nothing to be ashamed of, that all shame has left your body and been transmuted into love, pure love, golden love, which is flowing down from the heavens and pouring upon you, washing you clean.

Let it all wash you clean. Wash yourself clean of any regret you have over what you have done or not done. Let it wash you clean of any shame you feel about your own body and how you have felt. Let it wash you clean of shame and accept your passion, your passion about life, your passion within your body. Let it all flow and wash you clean and know that you are joined with the heavens within this body, and that this body is good, is pure, is nourishing, is a part of the melding and oneness which is your connection to life. Know this melding, this oneness, and accept it within you.

Take a pause and breathe.

And now, allow your focus to move down to the base of your spine, the seat of your security and centeredness. Know yourself here as stable and fully safe. Know that you are safe and surrounded by help at every turn. Know that you can create a life for yourself which blends all of this, blends the safety and security you need, your desire for love, your desire for excitement and a vibrant fulfilling life, with the deep truth within you, your loving heart and all of the senses of your body. Know that this is all one and all good. Know that as the spirit moves through you and fills you, as it moves down from the openness in the crown of your head, through your heart and to filling your entire body, that you can learn to take it all as one, you can learn to understand and feel how this body is precious and pure and an expression of the love that you are.

Take a pause and breathe.

Feel your readiness to share all of this, to share who you are with the world, to express yourself in all ways, through spirit, through action, through the integrity which moves your truth through your body, and lovingly, through your sensual, spiritual and sexual self. Know all of this as one and know that a love which combines all of this, a love which stems from your truth and your spirit, can find expression in your sexuality in a pure, loving and nourishing way.

You are love. Show it and be it. Know that the more you love yourself, the more you will be able to open to the love of others, open to receiving their love and giving love to them. Know that it all begins with this, this total acceptance and love of yourself. Know that you can do this, that you can learn to love yourself so deeply that the expression of this love outwardly will be natural and flowing, simply an outward and joyous expression of the beauty and love which flows within you, which is you, even now.

Take a pause and breathe.

As you go out in the world today, remember that your entire body is a pure and beautiful expression of your soul in this life. Remember to love yourself in all your glory, exactly as you are.

Soul

Take three steady, slow intentional breaths in and out, in and out, in and out. Please do this three times, consciously, slowly, and lovingly. Please put your hand over your heart and take three more slow and steady breaths in.

Become aware of the light glowing in your center. There is a light and it is you. It is completely you, the unique spark which is you. It is you, but it is also connected to the One that is all. And as you allow this spark to spread, as you give it full expression in your life, you will learn that you are a part of something larger than you, something that is you and that yet encompasses you, and you will begin to see how your spark is one with all that is, how your unique contribution to the whole is what makes it perfect and complete. You will begin to experience yourself as the note which makes the chord complete, as the piece which makes the puzzle whole, as the one unique touch which completes the picture of how all is and should be.

Your contribution is necessary. You are deeply important in every way. Your soul knows this and your light glows with what you are and are to become as you learn to express yourself with more and more fullness.

And so, begin with allowing this light to spread within you, this light of love, this light of soul. Allow it to spread and fill you. Feel the light moving to each part of your body, setting you aglow with the light of your higher self, your soul.

Take a pause and a breath.

And for a moment, just listen to what your soul wishes to tell you. Listen to the voice of your soul as it spreads within your body and tells you who you are and what you are to do. The language of your soul may be a feeling or a vision, it may be words in your mind, it may be a gentle knowing. However your soul wishes to speak to you, just let this language flow within you, let the message spread throughout your body.

Take a pause and a breath.

Move your focus to your heart. Still glowing all over with this message from your soul, move your focus to your heart and feel your courage. Feel it within you. Feel the courage growing within your heart, the courage to listen to your soul as it speaks to you, the courage to be who you are and do what it is that you must do. Feel your courage strengthening you and allowing you to listen to your soul as it speaks.

And if your soul's message is not clear, then strengthen and breathe into your heart. Know that you may be blocking your soul's message through fear. Acknowledge the fear and then release it, let it go. Let it go and fill that place with courage. The courage to listen truly to your soul as it speaks, to listen to your self and acknowledge what it is that you are meant to do with your life, what it is that you are meant to do right now.

You will not understand why. You will be called to move on faith and only on faith. You will be called to act out of a sense of rightness. You will be called to use every ounce of courage and faith in moving yourself forward from this place of confusion and tension, into the place of flow, where each step is shown to you just before it is taken, where your heart moves on courage and faith and the flow is felt but not known rationally or intellectually. You will be called from your heart, not your mind and not your ego. Go to this place within your heart where you can hear the call.

Take a pause and a breath.

And now, surrender. Surrender your will. Surrender the fight. Surrender the parts of you which want to fight and resist, the parts which need explanations, the parts which need to defend the old ways you have been. Surrender all of this to the message of your soul, the part which is telling you what you truly must do.

Today, perhaps you will only surrender a little piece, but it is a start. To listen to a little bit of your soul's message and to fill yourself with courage and then to surrender your own will to that of God; it is a start. It is a step.

And that is all that is needed. Just one step at a time. Just one little piece of faith to light the way. Just one little bit of courage of overcome yet another fear, one little bit of faith to overcome yet another doubt. Every day, with every step, a little more courage, a little more faith, all leading into surrender of the ego and mind, handing it all over to God's will, God's direction and that of your soul.

For your soul is the soul of God and your soul's voice speaks with the voice of God. Listen. Listen and you will hear. Listen and you will know that it is all one and good.

Take a pause and breathe. Open your heart, consciously.

Be one with these words:

I no longer confuse what I seem to be with Who I Really am. I still my mind and greet my courage. Here in my solitude I am not burdened by thoughts of the past. I have no fear of the future. I listen to the Voice of my soul inside me and I allow it to guide me to my life. I awaken to the sound of my life and feel my well-being as I place myself in the hands of the One Spirit, God. The Consciousness that brought my Spirit here is the Consciousness that will guide me through my life – safely. My path is illuminated with pure white light as I take my first step toward my authentic life.

Every question I have is met with an answer when I still my mind to listen. I trust in the message of my soul and my way is made clear. This day is the birth mother of tomorrow and I create my tomorrows by the choices I make today. I know that I am fulfilling the dream that was always meant for me as I take each step of my life forward with love and with courage.

I bend myself to positive faith and allow the Power for good to surge around me and through me. I charge myself with radiant I Am light, and embrace all Power given to me from above and below. My courage dispels the limits and inhibitions of my past. I will live each day from this moment on in accordance with the message from my soul and be lifted in to the future of myself. I am indeed blessed. And so it is.

As you go out into the world today, glow with the light that is you and surrender fully to the message of your soul. Radiate Bliss. **B**alance. **L**ove. **I**ntegrity, Sexuality, Soul.

Namaste,

Maureen Moss

About the Author

To arrange speaking engagements, retreats, workshops, or personal coaching, contact Maureen via email at maureen@maureenmoss.com or visit www.MaureenMoss.com

CPSIA information can be obtained at www.ICGtesting.com
Printed in the USA
BVOW05s2152130715

408661BV00019B/226/P